THE UNIVERSITY OF MICHIGAN
CENTER FOR SOUTH AND SOUTHEAST ASIAN STUDIES

MICHIGAN PAPERS ON SOUTH AND SOUTHEAST ASIA

Editorial Board

Alton L. Becker
John K. Musgrave
George B. Simmons
Thomas R. Trautmann, chm.

Ann Arbor, Michigan

STUDIES IN MALAYSIAN ORAL AND MUSICAL TRADITIONS

Music in Kelantan, Malaysia and Some of Its Cultural Implications   William P. Malm

* * * * *

Professional Malay Story-Telling: Some Questions of Style and Presentation   Amin Sweeney

Ann Arbor

Center for South and Southeast Asian Studies

The University of Michigan

1 9 7 4

Michigan Papers on South and Southeast Asia, 8

Open access edition funded by the National Endowment for the Humanities/ Andrew W. Mellon Foundation Humanities Open Book Program.

Library of Congress Catalog Card Number 74-83599

International Standard Book No. 0-88386-491-6

Copyright 1974

by

Center for South and Southeast Asian Studies
The University of Michigan

ISBN 978-0-88386-491-3 (paper)
ISBN 978-0-472-12828-0 (ebook)
ISBN 978-0-472-90228-6 (open access)

The text of this book is licensed under a Creative Commons Attribution-NonCommercial-NoDerivatives 4.0 International License: https://creativecommons.org/licenses/by-nc-nd/4.0/

CONTENTS

Music in Kelantan, Malaysia and Some of
Its Cultural Implications

      William P. Malm 1

Professional Malay Story-Telling:
Some Questions of Style and Presentation

      Amin Sweeney 47

MUSIC IN KELANTAN, MALAYSIA AND SOME OF ITS CULTURAL IMPLICATIONS

by

WILLIAM P. MALM

Kelantan is the northernmost province on the east coast of Malaysia. It is considered to be the most orthodox area in a nation whose state religion is Islam. At the same time it must be noted that it borders to the north with the Buddhist country of Thailand and to the west is the Malaysian province of Perak whose jungles and mountains contain many "pagan" tribal traditions. Beyond Perak is Kedah with its larger Indian and Chinese populations and to the south is Trengganu where some Indonesian traits are still to be found. English, Dutch, and Portuguese colonial periods in Malaysia have left their cultural souvenirs and modern versions of western fads are a natural part of Kelantan's mass communication and economic world. Viewed from afar, Kelantan would seem to be a culturally surrounded citadel of Islam in continental Southeast Asia. It is partly in this context that our study of its music will be made. First, however, we must review briefly the musical-cultural history of Malaysia in general.

The population of Malaysia consists of indigenous, Chinese, and Indian peoples, each of whom maintains their special musical castes. In some mountainous or jungle regions one finds tribes whose dream songs, bamboo instruments, jews' harps, and stamping tubes are similar to types found in similar locations all over the Southeast Asian mainland and its islands. Large bronze drums found in Pahang show that the Indochina Bronze Age was known in Malaysia by at least the first century A.D.

while trade with China and India seems to go back to the seventh
century B.C. Artisans and tradesmen from both these countries,
particularly China, were part of the Malayan scene throughout
all historical records thereafter though the major increases in
immigration occurred in the nineteenth century in the form of
labor forces for the developing tin and then rubber industries.
Both ethnic groups held to their earlier musical tastes so that
today one can hear in Malaysia vintage Chinese operas and
puppet dramas as well as Indian bangsawan musicals. Returning
to earlier times one can note that the ancient coastal kingdoms
of Malaysia reflected the economic and intellectual prestige of
Hinduism. Malayan chiefs certainly must have been aware as
well of the many other, larger Southeast Asian kingdoms in such
places as Indonesia, Cambodia, and Thailand. The east coast
of Malaysia seemed to be particularly connected with the Maja-
pahit kingdom of Java in the mid-fourteenth century. Under this
influence, many of the former Hindu kingdoms of Malaysia
became Moslem sultanates. In the sixteenth century the Portuguese took over Malacca and the Dutch and English soon followed
suit in trade and political influence. The intrepid Arab trader
left his mark in Malaysia as is evident in the zapin village dance
which is sung in Arabic in Malaysia to the accompaniment of the
l'ud and other Near Eastern instruments. The British domination
of the peninsula supported and controlled the various regional
sultanates so that, even after Malaysian independence in 1957,
the sultans of Kedah, Perak, Trengganu, Kelantan, and, now,
the King of Malaysia were able to maintain slight remnants of
Moslem court music. The musical marks of the colonial period
and modern mass communications were mentioned earlier.
With this brief background, let us turn now to Kelantan.

The tribal music to the west of Kelantan has little direct
influence on the coastal and plains peoples though we should note
the tradition of jungle dream songs and shamanism for reference
later. The influences of Thailand to the south are more obvious
and direct. For example, a Thai Lakon theatrical called Manora
is found in Kelantan and, on the west coast, in Kedah (Brandon,
1967, 61-62). The performers themselves are usually Thai and
the language they use can be a mixture. The accompanying
ensemble consists of two tacked-headed, stick-beaten barrel
geduk drums, two single-headed gedombak pot drums, two small
knobbed gongs set in a rack and/or wooden sticks which are
clacked together plus a serunai, double reed aerophone.

These instruments combine with actors to produce a type of theatrical available deep in the Buddhist world of continental Southeast Asia as far as Cambodia and Laos. At the same time one can note that the main actor is in the costume of a Manora bird, who is the major princess from a Hindu Sanskrit drama Divyavadana, which turned into the Buddhist Pali story Sudhana-jataka in Thailand. Traditionally the cast was all-male though today girls may be used. The serunai oboe and the earlier transvestite tradition of Manora might make some think of possible Islamic influence but the basic musical style, particularly the singing, is more typical of those musics heard elsewhere on the Southeast Asian mainland. Historically it would seem that Manora is an example of the confusion of trails that is part of any study in the cultural dynamics of Kelantanese arts.

Fight dances are popular throughout Southeast Asia, the Malaysian form (bersilat) seeming to be closer to the Indonesian style than to Thai boxing. The accompanying ensemble consists of one gong, two drums, and a serunai oboe. As in almost all of Southeast Asia, the gong is knobbed. The drums (gendang) are the equally common barrel drums with two lashed heads. A comparison of Kedah and Kelantanese performances, however, shows that performance practice is not always the same (Book Record [BR] item 1 & 2). The Kedah example is taken from a special videotape session in Kampong Padang Lumut, Kedah at a school of Javanese silat and Thai boxing. The teacher, who played the lead drum throughout the demonstration, said that his main teacher had come from Java. The Kelantanese example was recorded during one of the many public events going on at the sports grounds and stadium of Kota Bharu during the Sultan's birthday festival in 1968. The Kedah drums were played by hands with interlocking patterns in a Ma'yong style to be discussed later. The Kelantanese drummers hit the right hand head with a stick more in the style of the South Indian tavil (Jairazbhoy, 1970, 381-382). While a similar one-stick playing method can be found in Bali, the fact that the stick is curved outward seems significant since such an unusual beater has been found in the ancient Near East (Sachs, 1940, 249) while the sticks that curve inward towards the head are more common in parts of Africa (Ankermann, 1901, 61). Such single outward curving sticks are found in ancient India as well (Marcel-Dubois), 1941, Plate VIII) and can be seen on the thirteenth century bas reliefs of Angkor Wat in Cambodia (see the southern section of the west outer gallery). A general reader may find this detail picayune but it has been given to show how comparative musical organology (the science of music instrument studies) can often prove to be most useful in one's search for the relations between various musical cultures (Malm, 1967, 22-23).

The oboes in our two fight dance examples are also worthy of comparison. Both serunai are typical of related instruments found in most Southeast Asian fight accompaniments. The most indigenous aspect of such instruments seems to be the construction of their reeds. The reed is held freely ("swallowed") in the mouth and usually activated constantly through nasal breathing, two features common to many folk oboes. The unique characteristic of the serunai is the fact that each face of the reed has two plies, thus making it what might be called a quadruple double reed! This unusual arrangement gives the instrument its special tone quality. If the reeds are placed on the instrument at right angles to the mouth cavity, it is possible in addition to jump the pitch of one fingering up a fifth by "cutting out" the outer two plies of the reed with a raising of the tongue, a ticklish but efficient means of transposition. Field observations of the bersilat serunai have been limited but it was noted in the Kedah example that the bell of the instrument in Kedah was more conical than serunai used in other types of music heard in Kelantan. The shape of the instrument itself might reflect a Moslem influence, perhaps via India (Jairazbhoy, 1970) though the reed does not. However, it must be mentioned if only to contrast it with the pi chawa, an instrument of Javanese origin found to the north in the fight accompaniments of Thailand (Yupho, 1957, 81).

Excerpts from actual melodies of the Kedah and Kelantanese serunai are found in Example 1. Through the trills and ornamentations one can see in both a tendency to move gradually from one pitch emphasis to another. To give some idea of the order in which such tonal emphases may occur, the subsequent long notes in the Kelantanese version are outlined after the transcription of the first line. The cumulative effect of this continuous, elongated line throughout the entire fight dance can be appreciated when one remembers that, through nasal breathing, the melody never stops. It builds in intensity as the fight becomes more dramatic. The striking difference in

the two excerpts is, perhaps, the "exotic" opening section of the
Kedah version with its movements from C to C sharp to D.
Such "chromaticism" is quite lacking in the Kelantanese style.
This point is emphasized if we turn to Kelantanese puppet theatre
music.

Indigenous shadow puppetry (wayang kulit) is still very
popular in Malaysia as is evident in the Sweeney study. One can
see in addition Thai shadow puppets as well as Chinese hand
puppet plays. In Kelantan one occasionally finds a performance
of Javanese-style wayang. The music for this group implies a
slight Indonesian influence for the melodic instrument is a three-
stringed rebab bowed spike fiddle. A set of two to four small
knobbed gongs set in a frame is used extensively. Such small
gong sets are commonly used in Malaysian wayang kulit ensembles
as creators of an ostinato but the melodic instrument for them is
the serunai (Plate I). A set of small hand cymbals (kesi) are
used in both the Javanese-style and some Malaysian-style ensembles. Such instruments are common in theatrical musics
throughout South and Southeast Asia (for example, the tala or
the ching. See Marcuse, 1964, 94 & 506). The clacking sticks
of the Thai Manora music can be found in some Malaysian wayang
kulit music groups and in Kedah there are a few ensembles which
use Thai xylophones and pi-style double reed aerophones. Such
a variety of possible combinations is a reflection of the artistic
and economic flexibility of the Malaysian puppet master (dalang).
To survive, the dalang's show must match his own taste as well
as that of his audience. In this spirit popular songs may appear
derived from any source appropriate to the occasion. The
dalang in such cases may break tradition and sing while, at
least on the basis of one Trengganu experience, the instrumentalists may become a replying chorus in the style of Ma'yong (to
be discussed below). All these variations notwithstanding, one
can say that there is a basic ensemble for Kelantanese Malayan
puppetry (commonly called wayang siam!). This group is
similar to that of the Thai Manora and consists of a serunai,
one or two hanging gongs, a set of two to four small knobbed
gongs or cheap pieces of metal, two pot drums (gedombak),
one gendang drum (see above), and one or two sets of geduk
two tacked headed barrel drums played on one end with sticks.
Such a combination of a quadruple-double reed with percussion
is typical of most of mainland Southeast Asian puppetry and is
one of the major differences between mainland and Indonesian

performances, the latter more often using metallophones and
the gendang (Belo, 1970, 155-156; Kunst, 1949, I, 148). A few
aspects of the performance practice of a wayang ensemble in
Malaysia can be seen in Example 2, an excerpt from the piece
"Pancha ragam" recorded in Wakaf Bahru, Kelantan in August,
1968 (BR, item 2). Though Example 2 contains seven tones,
it has a pentatonic core (C sharp, E, F sharp, G sharp, B).
When Maha Risi opens the same play with a proper Moslem
invocation, his melody is purely pentatonic. The only noteworthy tonal change occurs when the demigods come down to
join him at which time the serunai changes the G sharp to a
G natural. A study of all other recorded examples from Kelantan
adds only an occasional use of a D natural to the scale of
Example 2. Even in the most tonally profligate moments,
Kelantanese puppet music seems more modal or pentatonic than
major-minor.

The rhythmic patterns for the drums, gongs, cymbals, and
clacking sticks in wayang kulit is generally in a straightforward
4/4 time as seen in measure 1 of Example 2. However, during
the overture period and in certain more active parts of the play
the geduk players, like their Manora counterparts, may suddenly
play a very exciting rhythmic contradiction of the type shown
from measure 2 onwards in Example 2. Two geduk players can
take turns in performing these bursts of rhythmic energy as they
do in similar Manora situations. Such a contrastive rhythm or
a "roll" in the drum music of wayang kulit is a standard cadence
pattern used to accompany the exits of characters, the figurines
moving away from the screen so that their shadows enlarge as
they disappear. The repertoire of stock pieces has yet to be
studied. It is used to accompany processions, fights, love
scenes, and the like. The dalang signals the beginnings and
endings of selections by prearranged puppet movements or the
clacking of a board attached to his leg. The musical response
to a signal for the end normally is marked by the rhythm pattern
shown in Example 3 played by the geduk under the final phrase
of a serunai tune appropriate for the dramatic occasion.

The serunai appears in ceremonial musics outside the
theatre. The rarest examples are those of the nobat (naubat)
ensembles used for special events by the sultans of Kedah,
Perak, Trengganu, Kelantan, and now the King of Malaysia.
Except for the ubiquitous Southeast Asian knobbed gong

the instruments used, such as the serunai oboe, nefiri trumpet, pairs of small kettle drums, and a barrel drum (see Sheppard, 1962, 8-11), are closely related to those of similar-named groups in India (Jairazbhoy, 1970, 377), the Near East (see Nauba in Farmer, 1929, 153), and North Africa (Chottin, 1938, 66). Nobat may have originally come to Malaysia from Indian Moslem courts. However, it is noteworthy that in India the ensemble has sometimes slipped into Hindu use while in Malaysia it has remained completely in the Islamic tradition.

A more plebeian and more viable ceremonial ensemble in North Malaysia is the gendang keling. Such a group can play for any kampong celebration but most often is employed for weddings or circumcisions, two distinctly Moslem events. Such groups are said to be used in Kelantan though an opportunity to record one there did not arise during the expedition of May-August, 1968. Example 4 (BR, item 3) is derived from a videotape of a group from Jabi in the Kota Star district of Kedah, shown in Plate II. The serunai recorded had a conical bell rather like that of the instrument transcribed in Example 1a. The rest of the group consisted of two drums and a transportable knobbed gong much smaller than those of the previous ensembles mentioned. Since the musicians move occasionally in processions the drums, though still called gendang, also are different. They consist of two strapped heads attached to a barrel body and suspended at chest level in front of the two players, like small bass drums in a marching band. Both heads are struck by sticks. The right hand stick is curved outwards like the stick used in bersilat drumming while the left hand one is novel in both its form and playing method. It is like a thin wand and is held downward in a closed fist like a knife. One hits the left head by quickly twisting the wrist inward. The left head is smaller and thus produces the highest pitch. Its tone is often shaped by closing the resonance of the right head with the fingers of the right hand. Though there is some exchange of parts, the two drums in general play the same rhythm patterns. Some are rather involved and the one in Example 4, while relatively simple and only one version upon which several variants are performed, is worthy of comparison with the advanced rebana pattern in Example 6. Note particularly the first two and last two beats of each.

The tone system of the melody is equally interesting when compared with the previous examples. Though the ornamentation and long pauses on selected notes are similar, the weighted scale approximation shown at the end of Example 4 reveals a pentatonic core very similar to the Indonesian pelog scale (Kunst, 1949, vol. I, 62). This core was found in the seven pieces recorded out of a repertoire which was said to be over twenty. The major differences in the recorded pieces is an occasional increase in chromatic passages which added a more Islamic sound. This piece seems to illustrate the acculturational nature of many of the Malaysian musical traditions. It is, in fact, the way in which Malaysian musicians have created their own mixtures of the sounds from encircling musical cultures that give their music its special charm.

Our study of instrumental music in Kelantan would be incomplete without mention of ensembles which do not use the serunai. One is the tempat kelapa or tempat nyiur which consists of a group of wooden keys approximately three feet in length. Like the keys of the Indonesian gambang, each key is kept in place on the resonator by one or two pins. A unique aspect of the Kelantan ensemble is that each key is mounted separately over a circular wooden "sound board" with an external diameter of nearly two feet and an internal hole of one foot. This in turn is attached to a rubber mounting which is like two inner tubes of the same dimensions. Museum examples have been seen constructed over halves of coconut shells or deeper wooden bodies. The smaller modern examples observed in 1968 were each played by two children who pounded on the same key with padded mallets to create a very simple interlocking resultant rhythm, usually of steady eighth notes (BR, item 4). The function of the wooden slabs is purely rhythmic as they are all of the same general pitch. This description is based upon one observation at the sultan's birthday and no facts concerning the origin of the group have been collected. As it was played mostly by children, it may be a recent school activity. In any case it is obviously far removed from the gamelan and xylophone traditions of other parts of Southeast Asia.

The tempat kertok group seems to be a training ground for our second novel example, the rebana ubi, as its sound boards are painted like the head of these larger instruments. The rebana ubi ensemble consists of a congregation of two sizes of very large single-headed drums from two to four feet in diameter (Plate III). The heads are attached to iron rings and placed over slightly conical barrel-shaped bodies three feet high made of very thick, heavy tree trunk. The skins are secured and tightened by rattan lashing encircling some twelve large wooden wedge-like pegs driven into the base area of the body. These pegs serve as a stand which holds the open end of the drum slightly off the ground. By their tension they also serve as controllers of tone quality. The rebana ubi are used on festive occasions and present an equally energetic though sometimes a bit more complicated resultant rhythm as that of the children's ensemble mentioned above (BR, item 4). One or two men take great pleasure in pounding the strong buffalo skins of each rebana ubi with padded wooden sticks. Exhaustion seems to be the major factor creating an end to a given rhythmic ostinato.

Considering the known extensive contact of the east coast of Malaysia with Indonesia it may be surprising to note the general lack of any large gamelan ensemble tradition in Kelantan. It was found in the late nineteenth century in Pahang and Riau and via a Sultanate marriage was moved to Trengganu (Sheppard, 1967, 149-150). In the latter location, one gamelan in the slendro tuning survives, primarily through the efforts of national support. Modern ensembles made up of a mixture of traditional instruments have also been formed in places like Kelantan through similar national or personal efforts. The only surviving implication of an older gamelan tradition in Kelantan is the tari ashek, a female court dance accompanied by a rack of three knobbed gongs plus drums and a hanging gong. Its entire basic melody, called "Lagu Juban," is shown in Example 5. It is played over a simple colotomic structure and the melodic instruments employ none of the fanciful polyphonic stratifications typical of Indonesia. Nevertheless, it has its straightforward charm and its historical significance, not only as a reflection of grander days but also as a relative of the kulintang traditions in the Philippines.

Before leaving instrumental music mention should be made of national social dances to be found in Kelantan. The two most popular are the joget and the ronggeng. Western dance band combinations may be used but historically the most interesting accompaniment is that of a violin, a tambourine (rebana), a hanging gong, and a singer. Such a group relates to a so-called

"Dodang Sayang" form of love song which, like the Javanese kronjong, was derived from Portuguese popular music style after the sixteenth century. The combination of a western violin with an Arab tambourine and the Southeast Asian gong is a perfect example of the potential flexibility of things in the music world. The presence of a singer in the group leads us to a study of vocal musics in northeast Malaysia.

Kelantan, as a Moslem heartland in Malaysia, should first be considered vocally in terms of its Islamic music. The most obvious example would seem to be the reading of the Koran and the calls to prayer. However, both these phenomena are really not germane except on a comparative basis since music is strictly forbidden in orthodox Moslem activities (see Anderson, 1971). Neither the calls of the priest nor the chantings of the Koran are considered to be music by most Islamic sects though the "tunes" of the calls to prayer are well-known to any infidel who happens to live downwind of the large amplifiers attached to better mosques and Koran "readings" are available on L P records (see Discography, item 4). In the Sufi sects of Islam, found in Kelantan and elsewhere, one can hear religious chants called berdzikir or dzikir which relate to traditions known in certain whirling dervish idioms found as far away as Turkey (Disc., item 3).

A more legitimate Moslem musical activity in Malaysia is the performance of some form of hadrah, songs in praise of the Holy Prophet. These songs are often in Arabic and are usually accompanied by the rebana, a single-headed drum with metal jingles in its frame. The obvious relation of this instrument to the Near Eastern duf was implied earlier. Hadrah music in Malaysia may be heard at weddings and other important events (Disc., item 1, side 1, band 8). It is performed by groups, traditionally all-male, in which each player may have an opportunity to sing a verse alone. The hadrah itself is not known today in Kelantan though Trengganu has a similar form called rodat. However, there is a distant relative in terms of performance practice in a secular music called in Kelantan zikirbarat or dikirbarat. Two groups of men compete on stage in singing verses at each other in a song contest much like those found all along the Mediterranean littoral from Spain and Italy to such islands as Malta. In Kelantan, the performance practice is usually call and response, each group repeating a line given first by their soloist.

A closer relative to the hadrah tradition in Kelantan is the so-called rebana kerching in which a group of men playing rebana face a group of young boys dressed in short caps and songkok hats who perform dance songs supposedly in Arabic. Such performances are used to accompany the bridegroom to the bride's house or in honor of some sultan or other well-to-do person. Example 6 is a comparative score of two rebana kerching songs transcribed from videotapes recorded in July, 1968 at the public celebrations held in honor of the Sultan's birthday (BR, item 5). Each song was first sung by the men with the simple rhythmic accompaniment shown in the score as Rebana I. As they finish the tune, the boys came in a fourth lower (the pitch at which the transcription was made) and at a faster tempo while the men played the more lively accompaniment shown in the transcription as Rebana II. In both songs the boys went through hand movements and eventually steps as they sang, though the opening was done in the kneeling position. The text seems to have been in Arabic but was beyond translatable recognition in this performance.

The comparative score shows interesting similarities between the two pieces. Though they are of different length (I, 128 beats; II, 104 beats) and start at a different point in the rebana four bar rhythm, note that the preparation for every third bar of the rebana pattern except for II, 15 is rhythmically the same. Another point of interest is the use of D sharp in I and F sharp in II as long note melodic tensions (see I, meas. 3 and 11 or II, meas. 9, 11, 13, 19). The final cadence on G sharp in I and F sharp in II will sound particularly exotic to western-trained ears. Though the general tonal system of the two tunes is obviously not western it also is not clearly Islamic. However, when the melodies are combined with the special nasal tone quality of the singing, the rather non-Southeast Asian rhythmic pattern on an Arab-derived instrument, and the costumes and performance gestures of the boys, the total effect hints strongly of the power of Islam in this particular musical tradition. One look at the photograph on page 480, Vol. II of Music in Java (Kunst, 1949, refer also to Vol. I, 379) will show that the source of this Moslem event, like many other elements of Malaysian culture, may be to the South rather than to the Near East. In either direction, the Islamic aspects are provocatively strong.

The most striking vocal music in Kelantan is found in
Ma'yong, a music-drama in which all the lead roles are played
by women while the comedians and musicians are male.
Apparently of Patani origin (Sheppard, 1969, 109) it is said to
have been introduced into the entertainment of the Kelantanese
nobility some two hundred years ago. Up until the 1920's it
was a major theatrical entertainment in the court but after that
time it was forced more and more to rely on public performances
The village audiences and the modern entertainment media
caused great changes in the repertoire and in the style and
frequency of performances. By 1968 there was not a Ma'yong
actress to be found in the court and the occasional public
performances were dominated not by teenage dancing and singing
girls but more by slapstick male comedians. A three-month
attempt to videotape the basic older repertoire (Sheppard, 1969)
in that year was based primarily on the memory and talents of
ten village women and eight men. The head of the group was a
former "star" actress and one of the women had been in a palace
group in her youth. The archival intent of the videotape expedition and the resultant frequency of performances during that
period created useful if unnatural circumstances. Instead of
giving two to a dozen performances a year, the actresses were
on stage for some thirty-four nights in a period of ten weeks
(no performances were allowed on the sabbath, Thursday night,
and other theatricals were recorded within the same field period)
For most of the actresses it was their first extended season and
they perforce became more trained. By the end of the last of
the ten plays (one play takes from two to five nights) they had
been noted even by the distant Ministry of Youth, Sports, and
Culture in Kuala Lumpur, and with the continual help of
Malaysia's most intrepid cultural enthusiast, Tansri Dato Haji
Mubin Sheppard, a small school for the training of new young
performers was founded. More important to this study is the
fact that good singers and musicians became better and the
author captured some ninety hours of their efforts which only
now has he begun to reassess.

Ma'yong takes place on an open stage some fifteen feet
square. It is raised three feet off the ground and covered by a
roof. All four sides are open although the "back" can be
screened off to lead to a dressing room and a low rail normally
is found along the open sides. Audiences can sit on the ground
on any open side and, if admission is charged, a tall palm frond
fence encircles the entire theatrical compound. At the outer
fringes of this area one may find coffee and food stands.

The first major event in the beginning of a Ma'yong play of any consequence is a blessing ceremony. If the patron is sufficiently affluent, special decorative strings of offerings may be hung from the cloth ceiling stretched beneath the peaked roof. Similar decorations may be found between the ropes suspending the two gongs in the stage right corner. One of the two gongs often contains a string of pennants (panji panji), raw cotton thread (a common defense against evil) and small figurines (semar and turas) of wayang kulit origin. A further magic power of the gongs can be found in a small pool of water in their rim in which singers often dip their fingers in order to coat their throats with power.

The power of the blessing ceremony lies in the hands and voice of a bomor who recites very long prayers protecting the troupe from all levels of danger in a manner quite like that noted years ago (Cuisinier, 1938: Part II, 129-187). He sits in the center of the stage with a large tray of food offerings plus a censer of smoking incense. Purifying candles are attached to the drums and gongs and placed beneath the stage. Each stage prop is cleansed in the incense smoke and eventually the rebab bowed lute and the two gendang drums are given to the bomor for blessing. Using a dish of rice from which occasional blessings have already been thrown, he moves his hand from the rice to the face of the drum and after some rubbing and a quiet prayer, strikes it three times, coats it with incense smoke, and moves on to the next drum. The gongs are blessed with smoke and gentle showers of rice after which the bomor returns to center stage for a secret prayer accompanied now by a nervous rebab prelude. The climax of this section of the blessing comes when the bomor begins to sway as if entering a trance. He suddenly throws a right hand fist of rice to the ground and over his shoulders while the gongs and drums enter along with the rebab in a dramatic accompaniment. The next fist of rice is held for half a minute to the bomor's mouth. He seems to suddenly blow at it (filling it with the breath of life?) after which it is flung to the ground and over the shoulders like the first round. A third round of this compelling movement is followed by three walks around the stage in which each area is properly purified by incense smoke while the ensemble plays an accompanying piece. Special attention is paid to a dish of offerings hanging at the front of the stage (for this ceremony only). Water is passed through the incense and then is sprinkled by

the bomor in turn on all the same props, instruments, and
stage areas. The music continues as the bomor packs his mat
and other paraphernalia and leaves the stage and the musicians
carry on with instrumental versions of Ma'yong pieces as an
overture to the actual performance some forty minutes later.

After the opening ceremony no further rituals are performed
unless some illness or other bad luck should arise during the
"season." However, it can be seen elsewhere as this form of
blessing is almost the same as one used by the dalang before
the start of a wayang kulit (see Singaravelu, 1969). Time has
been spent on the Ma'yong version of such an opening ceremony
not only because it is fascinating but also because it is filled
with a sacred power that is often unknown to casual viewers of
the theatrical itself. Though many of the modern performances
are slapstick or a bit ribald, the "classical" plays are still
treated by performers with a certain respect and fear. Names
and the plots of ten such plays can be studied (Sheppard, 1969,
110-113) though others have been recorded and many more may
still lie hidden in the oral tradition. Within this as yet indeterminate repertoire, many of the myths about rajas, princes,
and demons are "history" to some performers and the dangers
happening to characters are taken quite seriously. Proof of
this feeling is found in the fact that during the season of the
recordings bomor were used three times: at the beginning of
the season, at the change of location, and after a particular
scene of the play (Dewa Muda) in which a prince is killed. The
feeling of dread among the actresses must have been sincere
as the author did not pay for the extra protective ceremony.
The degree to which the magic side of Ma'yong is native or
Islamic is difficult to say at this point of the research. Most
of the prayers were in Malayan though Arabic words did appear.
Cuisinier has already pointed to some of the interesting mixtures
of traditions in similar ceremonies (1936) and, though more
needs to be done in Malaysian ritual research, we must turn
now to the basic area of this study as found in Ma'yong: its music

We have already become somewhat familiar with the
instruments of the Ma'yong ensemble via our description of the
opening ritual. In our musical study let us turn first to a few
more details concerning the instruments themselves. The two
double-headed barrel drums are called gendang, a name parallel
with that of similar drum pairs found in Indonesia. The drum

bodies are usually made of jackfruit wood and the larger head of each drum is made of cowhide while the smaller one is goatskin. As seen in Plate IV, the higher-pitched small head is normally played with the left hand. Note in the picture how the skins are encircled by split bamboo pieces and secured with rattan. The larger drum is called the ibu (mother) and the smaller anak (child).

The two gongs (tawak-tawak) hung in the stage left corner have already been described in terms of their magic content. All that need be added is that they are placed with their knobs facing inward toward one another so that the player can easily hit one or the other. Their pitch varies from a minor third to a fourth apart. The rebab-bowed lute is perhaps of greater interest for the distribution and physical variety of instruments of this name is very great in the Moslem world (Marcuse, 432, 436-438). The Ma'yong variety as seen in Plate IV is larger than its nearby Indonesian relative and has three strings (the Javanese use two). Their standard tuning is in two fourths. The pitch is influenced by the singers or the gongs. A fourth and fifth tuning may also be used. The strings once were twisted cotton but now guitar strings are usually used instead. The wooden body has a cow's stomach or a buffalo skin face upon which a small wax nipple (susu) is placed in the upper left area to mute the tone. The high wooden bridge is placed in the center of the face near the nipple. In Kedah to the northwest one can occasionally find a Ma'yong rebab with a coconut shell body and two cotton strings in the style of the saw duang of Thailand (see Yupho, 1960, 102) but the three-string variety described above is most typical of Kelantan today. Its long bow is made of handsomely filigreed teakwood and strung with coconut palm fiber, violin bow strings, or Chinese fish line.

The serunai double reed is used in only one dance, the Tari Ragam, in Ma'yong and is borrowed from the puppet and the Manora tradition so need not be studied further here. The other major musical resources are the solo singers and their responding chorus but let us start our musical discussion first with the overture music in which only the instruments are used.

Before every evening of a performance, the musicians play some 45 minutes of instrumental versions of selected standard vocal pieces such as Saudara shown in Example 7 (BR, item 6). Such music may start with a short rebab prelude though it does not in this case. Example 7 begins at the moment of the entrance of the percussion for it is felt that a study of one example of full ensemble music will reveal several important principles basic to all Ma'yong music. To understand such principles it is best to begin by conceiving the music as consisting of three layers of events, each different in sound and in rhythmic density. The most tonally and rhythmically dense is the melodic layer, in this case the rebab. The section of the melody transcribed shows a core of four notes (B, C#, D#, F#) from a standard pentatonic plus an E as a trill in measure 3 and a D natural as a kind of "blues third" ornament in measure 5. However, the rhythmic variety evident in this first section shows how such a restricted tonal vocabulary is kept from being dull.

The least active in both tone and rhythm is the gong part, its two pitches being indicated by the letter G for the upper pitch (D sharp in this case) and the lower pitch (B) by a G with a downward arrow. Anyone familiar with Southeast Asian music will recognize that the gong part forms a colotomic structure, that is, it divides the music into temporal units by the regular entrance of specific sounds in a specific order on specific beats. Note how the cadence is announced by the greater intensity of the gong part in measure 8.

The two interlocked drum parts add the vital third layer between the other two. The casual western viewer, watching the drummer play such compelling rhythms without the standard western crutches of a conductor, notation or even the visual contact of string quartet players might be mystified by the way in which the drummers can combine their two parts into the kind of exciting resultant rhythm only partly realized in the notation of Example 7. The secret of these parts lies in the use of various rhythmic patterns of sixteen or eight beat lengths. Two such patterns appear in the transcription (marked as I and II) though the entire piece uses five different units. Like good dixieland or bluegrass musicians, the drummers are able to vary basic patterns without losing track of the ever-increasing tempo or of the primary elements of each pattern. Example 8 illustrates how this is done by comparing pattern II of the transcription with its variants in the next double period of the piece (included on the record).

With the three layers in mind we can turn now to the structure of the entire piece as outlined below. The six sections of the piece are marked by Arabic numerals. After 8 beats of somewhat free rhythm the piece enters into a steady beat which becomes faster in each section from approximately mm 82 at the beginning to nearly mm 200 by the end. In the midst of this increasing tempo one of the most charming patterns is III which utilizes a fast dialogue between the drums at a suddenly softer volume. The first entrance of this pattern in section 3 is made all the more interesting by the use of the lower gong in a totally different manner as seen in Example 9. The standard colotomic structure is shown in 9A and the gong part of section 3 in 9B. Since the lower gong signals major cadences in every other case its tone is changed in this selection by muffling the gong's resonance with the player's hand.

Structural Outline of Saudara

	1.	2.	3.
Rebab tonal emphasis	B C# B	C# B	D# B
Drum patterns	I II	I' II' II' II'	III III III III
Length in beats	32	64	64

	4.	5.	6.
Rebab tonal emphasis	B C# B	C# B	F# B
Drum patterns	IV IV IV IV	III III III III	V IV
Length in beats	64	64	32

The lower gong is not the only indicator of sections. Note how the tonal emphasis of the rebab changes at the start of each double period. In this context note also that the high F# is not emphasized until the start of the final section and a cadence signalling drum pattern (V) appears at the same time. This section balances the overall structure of the piece by being the same short length as the beginning (32 beats). Put all together the section lengths, the tonal signals of the rebab, the colotomic structure of the gong part, and the drive of the drum patterns create a sense of musical tension and release in a way equally logical if totally different from that found in western or other non-western musics. Such necessary logical elements are found as well in the vocal music of Ma'yong.

The instrumental overture period is over when the cast
arrives to the accompaniment of a <u>Barat</u> piece (Disc., item 2,
side 1, band 1). Once the cast is on stage the women involved
in a given play sit in rows facing what could be called stage
front, the rebab player facing them. Comedians and excess
actresses tend to sit along the opposite side from that of the
instrumentalists or at the back of the stage. The plot, musical
content, and length of the plays may vary greatly but it is usually
easy to identify the actresses playing rajas, princes or female
royalty by their costumes, which are often based on the fashions
of the late nineteenth century Kelantanese court. Musically all
plays begin with the same piece, <u>Mendagap Rebab</u>, an excerpt
of which is found on the Book Record (item 7 and Disc., item 2,
side 1, band 3. See Plate IV). The title means to face or honor
the rebab. Its text, like that of Malaysian <u>selampit</u> storytellers,
tends to start with a standard statement like "This is a story of
a king in a land..." Such an opening phrase is not surprising in
storytelling anywhere in the world, but the musical style of this
example is truly a shock to old Southeast Asian hands (and ears).
The tune (<u>lagu</u>) begins with a very long, melismatic prelude
(the <u>kepala lagu</u>) played in a free slow rhythm by the rebab.
The percussion section eventually joins in a restrained manner
somewhat like pattern I of Example 7. All these characteristics,
like those of the instrumental overture pieces, are not unusual
in Southeast Asia. However, when the vocal part begins, the
musical plot thickens greatly. The voice and the rebab relate
heterophonically, that is, they are both giving different versions
of the basic melody at the same time. This is a very typical
Near Eastern tradition (see Malm, 1967, 41, 53). At the same
time the tonal structure becomes extremely ambivalent.
Example 10 gives the outline of the tonal vocabulary but a few
minutes spent with Item 7 of the Book Record
will convince the sensitive listener that western five line notation,
even with the best intended diacritical markings, will not ade-
quately represent the pitch inflections of the rebab or particularly
of the singer. In the modern parlance one might say that the
Gutenberg galaxy has been musically shattered, not by a Scotsman
(McLuhan) but by an unknown Arab: the one that brought the Near
Eastern musical tradition to Kelantan. The doubting Thomas
need only proceed to the chorus entrance in the period that
follows. Heterophony, that bothersome concept in ethnomusicology, slips into an even more involved form of polyphony, the
existence of more than one part of music, as against the

monophonic (single line) melodies we have viewed so far (note that we are referring to melody not rhythm at this point). Perhaps we must invent a new word like disphony (a Latin-Greek combination): multiple independent parts which may or may not be thematically related (Malm, 1972). In the West we call this counterpoint, in Kelantan they don't call it anything; they just sing it. The most germane point is that singing following this same unique form of multipart music can be heard in the Near East (Disc., item 7, band 2) more often than in Asia though the Kelantanese source may turn out to be Sumatra. Add the occasional vocal ullulation (yodel) heard in Ma'yong and a search for Islamic influence in Malaysia would seem to have come to a musical Mecca.

How kind of the native tradition to provide such clear cases in the first piece of every play, but what of the rest of the performance? On the basis of ninety hours of videotape it would seem that most Ma'yong music contains these same characteristics though some are not so aggressively Moslem as the first piece. On this presumption let us look next at the actual size of the musical repertoire of the genre. A study of eleven different plays produces the names of over thirty tunes. The titles listed below (alphabetically) are either the most frequent or of special interest. To indicate their use, the number of appearances of each piece in four different plays of different lengths is included. The code for these plays is as follows:

```
RML   Raja Muda Lembek, "The Broken Vow"      1 night
GB    Gading Bertimang, "The Magic Elephant"  2 nights
RTH   Raja Tangkai Hati, "The Spell of the
                                    Giantess" 3 nights
ARG   Anak Raja Gondang, "The Triton Shell
                                    Prince"   5 nights
```

BARAT. The name of this tune means west which in Kelantan means from Thailand. It is the standard exit, entrance, or action music and is often played with little or no vocal part at all. It comes in different styles like Barat Anjor (spread out), Chepat (quick) or Kesah (anxious) Barat. From the statistics it is evident that Barat is to the Ma'yong what recitative is to western opera. RML, 11; GB, 38; RTH, 49; ARG, 110.

BERJALAN. The title means to walk along and think. It is found in puppet play music as well as in Ma'yong. It normally leads into the Tari Ragam dance listed below. RML, 1; GB, 1; RTH, 1; ARG, 5.

DANDONGDAN. The title refers to the nonsense syllables often used by the Ma'yong chorus. Extra terms like chingit (shrill) refer to the singing style while lenggan (swaying the head and body) or tonggek (stick out the buttocks) refer to the dance. The word kasidah is also found which refers to an Arab form of music. RML, 1; GB, 2; RTH, 1; ARG, 6.

JAMBAR. Though rare, this title is of interest as it is the name of a line of Rajas. The original Raja Jambar or Jembal is said to have come out of a bamboo node and his descendants founded the village Jambal near Bachok, Kelantan. One of the Rajas (all children of a Sultan may be called Raja or Tengku) was said to have been a good musician some thirty years ago. The Puteri shaman claim him as much as the Ma'yong performer RML, 1; ARG, 1.

KIJANG EMAS. The title means the golden mousedeer. The title is found in the Javanese-style shadow theatre of Kelantan as well, though the tune may be different. The title may be derived from a scene in the Kelantanese version of the Ramayana in which Ravana or his sister turn into a deer. In other Malayan and Indian versions of the story, it is a servant that turns into a deer (Zieseniss, 1963, 44). RML, 3; GB, 4; RTH, 4; ARG, 14. (Disc., item 2, band 4)

MENGADAP REBAB. This piece is listed here for alphabetical reasons and has already been discussed above. It is used at the start of every play and the only time it appeared twice was when the location of performances changed before a play was finished, Bongsu Sakti ("The Flying Apeskin") in this case.

MENGAMBUL. The title means for something to ricochet but the function of the piece is to accompany a scene of sadness or weeping. GB, 3; RTH, 3; ARG, 7.

MENGULEK. A generic term for various lullabies and accompaniments for bathing princesses or throwing flowers. Many of the songs in this genre are well known and sung outside the context of the plays unlike most of the rest of the music. (Disc., item 2, band 1). RML, 2; GB, 2; RTH, 3; ARG, 9.

PA'YONG MUDA. This song obviously occurs in the proper dramatic situation as its title means the young prince. RML, 1; GB, 1; RTH, 2; ARG, 7.

SAUDARA. The title means a relative and the song texts refer to a brother or a friend. RML, 1; GB, 2; RTH, 4; ARG, 6.

SEDAYONG. Some eight different pieces in this genre are found. Some are titled in relation to who is singing such as Sedayong Pa'yong (prince or raja), Ma'yong (the queen, hear Item 2, side 1, band 5), Puteri (princess), Peran (comedian) while others refer to the style of the music or the dance Chingit, Tonggek, or Manja. One relates to a Moslem influence with the combination Sedayong Mamat, the local word for Mohammed. The original meaning of the word sedayong is not yet known. RML, 3; GB, 8; RTH, 2; ARG, 22.

SINDONG. The title remains a puzzle though its use is common. RML, 1; GB, 3; RTH, 2; ARG, 3.

TARI RAGAM. Ragam in Malayan usually refers to a pattern rather than a melody and tari refers to dance. Thus the title would seem to refer to a dance pattern. As mentioned earlier, the piece is derived from the Thai Manora tradition with its use of clacking sticks and the serunai oboe (hear Disc., item 4, side 2, band 10). The choreography is also derivative from Manora for it is the only Ma'yong dance which moves in a slowly accelerating figure eight floor pattern. RLM, 1; GB, 1; RTH, 2; ARG, 1.

TO'WAK. The song title relates to its use for it usually appears in a play as an "old man's" song. (Disc., item 4, side 2, band 2). RTH, 1; ARG, 5.

YUR. The meaning of the word is not known but the piece is always sung by a clown or at the end of a play if a Barat is not used (Disc., item 4, side 2, band 3). RLM, 2; GB, 1; RTH, 4; ARG, 2.

Having reviewed the music of Ma'yong in general and listed some of the most common melodies used in the tradition it is time that we look at one specific example of how such materials fit in an actual play. Our choice will be Gading Bertimang ("The Magic Elephant") as it was videotaped in Kok Pasir, July 26 and 27, 1968. An excerpt from the opening Mengadap Rebab has already been discussed above. This piece is followed in the July 26 performance by three circle dances: Sedayong Ma'yong, Kijang Emas, and Sedayong Pa'yong. Though it takes some twenty minutes to perform these first four dances they are unrelated to the plot of the play. The same numbers began each play observed and may relate to earlier ritualistic origins or to the desire of the troupe to appear classic or to prolong the play. Perhaps the function of such a beginning is to lull the audience into a receptive mood for the long drama that is to follow. The slow motion of each dance, reminiscent of Javanese classical styles, would certainly contribute to such a goal though most of the dances throughout a play are performed in a similar manner. The opening Mengadap Rebab is the only dance done in the sitting and squatting positions, all other (except Tari Ragam) moving in a slow circle (discussed below) with limited foot movements and delicate finger motions. Those familiar with the flashier Balinese and Thai dance traditions would find Ma'yong choreography quite different and perhaps puzzling, considering its survival in a folk tradition only. It is too early to say whether it represents a maintenance or a decay of earlier court theatre, but it is characteristic of contemporary village Ma'yong. In the Gading Bertimang play, the dances are followed by three forms of Barat which lead the raja, his wife, and other nobility to a moment of lament, handled musically by a Mengambul.
At this point the audience is informed that the wife of Raja Besar had two sons, both of whom disappeared soon after birth. When the third child, a girl, was born the queen betrothed it to a magic white elephant on the basis that the child should survive. All this dialogue is offset by the use of a Saudara, a Barat, a Sedayong Manja, and a special melody called <u>Lagu Elar</u> or <u>Berkhabar</u> which means to bring news at which point the raja says that he plans to marry his daughter instead to a son of another raja at the river mouth. A Sindong and two Barats change the scene and allow the princess to enter, now a grown girl of sixteen. She performs a fine dance to Sedayong Ma'yong followed by a Dandongdan Siduk. She asks her father for permission to go to the forest and Kijang Emas is used to get there

followed by a Berjalan and an entertaining Tari Ragam dance which has nothing to do with the play except to show the terpsichorean talent of the princess and her court. A travelling Barat takes the ladies to a pool where a Mengulik is performed based on the tune Kudang Bunga outlined in Example 10. The Book Record (item 8) gives the listener some idea of how the court ladies gambolled about the pool while the princess was properly washed. A study of the tune shows that it is much closer to the Malayan or Indonesian popular or folk song tradition, a logical source for a piece of music in this theatrical situation. The outline of the tune shows that even western popular music may have left its mark on the last two bars.

With a Barat the scene changes and a missing son of the raja appears. With another Barat he puts on an elephant skin and via Barat flies down to the area where the princess is bathing. Because of the special double aspect of the role, it is played by a comedian instead of an actress. Barat is heard as the girls start home but the elephant interrupts the procession and carries the princess away. With a weeping Mengabul, the ladies inform the raja that his daughter has been captured by a white elephant and at that tense moment a Barat brings the evening to a close for there must be a reason for the audience to return the next night (which they did). The audience, by the way, was quite large (approximately 800) as the author was paying for the show and thus there was no entrance fee. Enterprising sweets and coffee sellers established their stands without the fees normally due the entrepreneur but the author, having malaria at the time, stuck to his own boiled water for refreshment.

The second night began with the dance Sedayong Ma'yong, two Barats, a great deal of comedy, and another Barat which led to a Kijang Emas travelling song. This was followed by an older man's To'wak, a Barat leading to a Sedayong Tongget, a Sindong, and finally a Saudara at which point the story began again as the clowns go to see the white elephant. With a Barat the elephant enters and a Mengabul gives the princess an opportunity to lament her sad fate. In two different Barat passages the two clowns fight the elephant, unsuccessfully of course, and via a Barat go to the raja to tell him of their failure to rescue the princess. By this time, one hour of the evening has passed by pleasantly. The servants' report of the battle with the elephant is full of bravura and humorous lies and eventually the raja and his attendants form a circle for a performance of Kijang Emas.

At this point let us pause for a moment to understand how
the music enters into the tale. The rebab opening (kepala lagu)
of the Kijang Emas is covered by clown dialogue while the raja-
playing actress stands near the rebab facing center stage to
begin her solo section of the piece. She does not move during
this lyrical melismatic section though the clowns make slight
comic walking gestures. When the chorus enters in its disphonic
style the main actress begins to actually dance slowly turning
clockwise in such a way that many of her gestures are in the
direction of the rear of the stage or toward the musicians on
stage left. This curious manner of dancing out of view of stage
front is quite typical of Ma'yong choreography and possibly may
relate to some ancient courtly practice in which the royalty sat
at a different side of the stage from that of the common viewers.
As the dancer moves slowly in a circle counterclockwise around
the stage the two clowns jog along behind or in front of her.
By the time her second solo verse has come she is standing in
the stage right corner facing center and once more does not
move while singing, her journey beginning again when the chorus
takes over. Each of these solo and choral sections is the same
length as the structure of the instrumental version of Saudara
shown on page 17 (a version of the piece may be heard on Disc.,
item 4). The drum accompaniments and the gong cadence
signals are also the same. When the next solo section begins
the tempo has become slightly faster though the dancer stops
moving again. The final chorus section is yet a bit faster and
the piece closes with a half length coda of still quicker speed.
Thus, the form of the piece follows the typical outline shown
earlier with Saudara.

The plot resumes briefly as the raja instructs the servants
to call for the princess' fiancé and off they go to a Barat followed
by a Sedayong Ma'yong sung and danced with less style by one
comedian. After a short dialogue and another Barat they greet
the fiancé, a new actress in the play so far, dressed in a male
costume not unlike that of the raja. The fiancé, a young prince,
sings a pledge to save his would-be bride from the elephant with
a Dandongan Chingit and via Barat goes to visit the raja who
discussed the problem further with him. With the song Sedayong
Tongget the clowns lead the young prince on his way and call
forth the elephant who enters with the princess behind him as
his captive. The queen and the young prince tell the clowns how
to fight the elephant and the elephant and princess parade by them

with a Barat made more heavy by the use of clacking sticks in
the Manora style. Three Barats follow as first the clown and
then the queen, and finally the young prince try to destroy the
elephant without success (BR, item 9). The degree of skill in
the clown's battle is evident in the recording where one can hear
the audience's laughter as the elephant first hits him in the rump
with his trunk and then chases him up on the railing near the back
pillar of the stage. The elephant is made a white elephant, by
the way, by wearing grey clothes and a white turban which dangles
in front of him like a trunk (Plate V). A Barat signals the
fleeing of the three defeated people and the clown is instructed
to provide a boat which he does by lifting, with great effort, a
small wooden frame used to hold small gongs in Wayang-style
music. The queen and he turn their wooden swords into oars and
they paddle the young prince back to the sultan's palace for a
further parley. The raja now talks to his other servant and
sings a Sindong expressing the problem as well as providing
another classical circle dance in the form of the Kijang Emas
described above. This servant goes to the elephant via a Barat
and tries to talk him out of the princess as the raja has insisted
on a human groom. Barat brings the servant back with a report
of failure and the raja sings one of the lyrical Mengulek songs,
"Timang Welu," which does much to show her vocal ability but
little to further the plot. He (she) gets quite angry with his
inefficient servants much to the delight of the audience, for
royal figures always carry a whisk with which to strike the
servants in the style of Punch and Judy shows. The servants take
off with a Barat and visit once more with the queen and young
prince. They are involved in a very long dialogue which reveals
that the raja has offered the princess to anyone who can kill the
elephant. Such information is set in a matrix of endless jokes
and comic accents. Every time the characters move about
stage a short Barat can be heard and such music ends the funny
but dramatically irrelevant scene.

At last the plot moves forward as a new actress comes on,
covered with a shawl and peasant dress. She identifies herself as
the other lost son of the raja and with a Barat moves to the
musicians' side of the stage where she sits down and makes herself a simple turban and wraps the shawl around her ankle to
show that she is disguised as a crippled beggar. While she is
busy with this stage operation the rebab is busy retuning as he
knows that this actress sings at a higher pitch. She explains

her intentions with a Pa'yong Muda of somewhat shorter than
normal length. After her solo section the chorus enters as she
dances, again to the rear of the stage first in traditional fashion,
and then she stands still for her second solo. During the next
chorus entrance she sits and rubs her leg as if she were in pain
and chases flies away from her open sores. A half-length fast
coda ends the piece as the servants walk by, looking for a likely
hero to kill the elephant. Another long comic dialogue follows
between them and the beggar. They hold their noses at the smell
and are plagued by flies from the sores. The beggar demands to
fight the elephant but one servant describes the monstrous size
of the elephant in great detailed gestures that take little knowledg
of Kelantanese dialect to understand. A servant via Barat runs
to tell the raja of the strange request and the raja sends him back
via Barat to fetch the beggar. The latter insists on a cart to
carry him and the little gong frame, that was a boat not long ago,
is now brought over as a cart. The actual cart is formed by the
arms of two clowns and to the howling laughter and whistling of
the audience the "cripple" is taken to the palace with a Barat.
The slapstick action is completed when the servants drop the
beggar just as they get to the raja. After further dialogue the
cart is reformed and the beggar is carried off with a Barat to
meet the elephant who with a Barat (and the princess behind him)
enters the stage. Dialogue between the two secret brothers leads
to a short Barat-accompanied fight after which the elephant broth
takes off his trunk and elephant skin, discusses the rest of their
scheme, and departs. The skin is shown to the servants and one
throws it off stage with a Barat. The beggar and the princess
walk arm in arm to the palace via Barat. The beggar can claim
the princess as his bride but in a long dialogue explains that he
and the elephant are the lost sons who have done all this to allow
their sister to marry the young prince. The son leaves via a
Barat and the young prince is placed next to the princess and
betrothed by the raja. Then the raja, princess, prince, and
two clown servants dance the finale Barat whose words
traditionally say something like "The show is over and it is time
to go to bed. Each one go to their room but not someone else's
room." The actors kneel facing stage front and place their hands
together in the traditional Southeast Asian greeting or farewell
while the gong strikes several times to signal the end of the
evening. In two nights and some five hours the difficult situation
has been solved (in about fifteen minutes) and everyone lived
happily ever after. The actors must change, the audience carry

the sleeping children home, and the recorder pack up his 250 pounds of equipment for the next night and another play.

A review of this outline of one play shows how music and dance entertainment have been joined by extensive comedy to fill a simple folk tale with a variety of theatrical events. Music and classical dance were more frequent in the earlier hours of the play and when the plot had to be dealt with seriously, the musical section was reduced to an endless series of Barats. Their musical value may seem low but their theatrical use is dramatically logical. Ma'yong is folk theatre and what might seem gauche in a playhouse is totally successful in a village open theatre set in a coconut grove. The form of the important vocal pieces has been shown to be consistent and the relation of the solo singer to the rebab and the chorus parts to each other have implied a strong Islamic influence. At the same time the drum and gong accompaniments speak of common Southeast Asian traditions. All these factors placed with the costumes, the folk tales, and social setting of Ma'yong produce an excellent example of a creative eclecticism which is the life blood of peasant culture anywhere in the world. A Mummer's play of England will never replace Shakespeare and an old French lady singing a historical romance will never fill a theatre as well as Bizet's "Carmen." By the same token Ma'yong in its present style, probably a long way from its ancient palace form, can go on an international exchange tour only at the cost of losing its real charm: that of genuine folk theatre being done for folk minds and sense of humor. The archival expedition has captured some of this on videotape but let us hope that the resultant publicity and sudden temporary financial increment do not cause a pleasant native plant that basks under moonlight and kerosene lamps to change into a cheap plastic flower covered with sequins and sparkling under klieg lights.

A discussion of the musical-theatrical world of Kelantan cannot be complete without a view of Puteri or Putri, one of the shamanistic traditions of the coastal area. The dream songs of tribal Southeast Asia were mentioned earlier as part of the indigenous culture of the jungle (Disc., item 1). One of the fascinations of the more coastal agricultural Putri is the degree to which it may combine native paganism with Islamic magic medical aid. Cuisinier's study of 1938 (pp. 92-112) implies that Putri was used in courtly life as much as, if not more than,

in the village for many decades. With the demise of court life
this cannot be said today but the ceremonial equipment, offerings,
texts, and rituals used now are found to be hearteningly similar
to those studied over thirty years ago. The yellow rice, boiled
egg, fish net thread, and Javanese coins found on platters or
hung from the rafters in Bachok in 1968 match earlier descriptions. A small coconut placed on one pillar was a <u>sako</u>, a coconut to feed the genies. In general one seems to find a setting
not unlike that of the bomor ceremony that blessed the Ma'yong
stage in our earlier discussion. Our Putri setting was unnatural;
it took place in a gazebo in the daytime for videotaping rather
than in a hut at night for illness. However, so many factors
germane to the interest of this study appeared that the details of
the ceremony, its equipment, and its text will be left for the
reader to study in Cuisinier's writing in order that we can look
and listen to its music (BR, band 10).

To appreciate the style of Putri music one must first realize
that its function is to place the Putri bomor in a trance and let
the spirit enter him or her in order that the nature of a given
illness can be found out. To do this there must be an assistant
who can converse with the spirit in the bomor and discover the
problem. Normally this role is taken by a rebab musician who
plays facing the shaman. In addition he sings duets with him and
is the essential "straight man" in all the conversations. The
rest of the musical ensemble used today consists of two gendang
drums, Ma'yong style, a double gong player, and a performer
who strikes one or two relatively small turned over brass bowls
(batil) with thin sticks. The sound of these bowls is one of the
characteristic differences between the musical ideals of Ma'yong
and of Putri. The other striking difference is equally evident
on the Book Record (item 10). It is the vocal style. A female
shaman example was chosen so one could compare it with our
earlier Ma'yong examples. The tone system is unique (Example
11) but the low, throaty voice and flamenco-like vibrato at the
opening of the song seem miles away from the heterophony of
Ma'yong despite the similar instrumental accompaniment. The
occasional call of encouragement from other colleagues and
later, in the faster example, the alternate sections sung by the
rebab player and the dancing shaman are also vastly different
from the exchanges of solo and disphonic choruses in Ma'yong.
A study of the videotapes would show that the dance movements
are also different. Hip movements, sudden lifts of the leg, and

quick arm motions are most notable. Even without seeing such action, the reader can catch some of the style of the essential ceremonial moment in the lupa dance shown in Plate VI. The singing suddenly stops and the batil playing becomes more intensive. During this time the shaman twirls his or her head violently until a trance is obtained. This event is uniquely Putri in Kelentan though many of the other pieces are derived by name or sometimes by tune from Ma'yong. For example, in Putri performances recorded the following titles appeared: Kijang Emas, Pa'yong Muda, Sedayong Ma'yong, Sedayong Pa'yong, Yur, and even Mengambul. Jambar, as implied earlier, is considered by some to be originally a Putri piece "stolen" by Ma'yong. The lupa sections of any piece are clearly in the Putri tradition only, but one can wonder how much of that tradition is indigenous. The trance-inducing hala section with the spinning head was once described by an informant as being "like a zar in trance dances from Egypt" and the reader is perhaps aware of the whirling dervish tradition of Turkey (Disc., item 5). The ritual materials and activities of Putri itself, such as sucking illness out of a patient after possession of a spirit, place it more clearly in the context of indigenous Southeast Asian culture but the vocal style, some of the accompaniment, and the means of inducing a trance by head whirling seem to be adumbrations of an Arab finger pointing towards the Near East.

Further field work and study in general Islamic and Southeast Asian shamanism will be needed before any conclusions can be reached concerning the background of Putri. In the same context each description given above of other musical genres in Kelantan specifically and Malaysia in general calls for extensive further work. Hopefully, this preliminary survey will tweak the curiosity of future ethnomusicologists so that more of the fascinating world of Malaysian music may become better known beyond the borders of its many musically rich provinces.

BIBLIOGRAPHY

Anderson, Lois
1971 "Religious Music of Islam," in *Music and History in Africa*, K. Wachsmann, ed. (Evanston, Illinois: Northwestern University Press), pp. 146-157.

Ankermann, Bernhard
1901 *Die afrikanischen Musikinstrumente*. Ethnologisches Notizblatt, Band III, Heft I (Berlin: von Haack), 189 pp.

Belo, Jane
1970 *Traditional Balinese Culture*. (New York: Columbia University Press), 421 pp.

Blacking, John
1954 "Musical Instruments of the Malayan Aborigines," *Federation Museums Journal*, Vols. I & II (Kuala Lumpur), 35 pp.

Brandon, James
1967 *Theatre in Southeast Asia*. (Cambridge: Harvard University Press), 370 pp.

Chottin, Alexis
1938 *Tableau de Musique Marocaine*. (Paris: Geuthner), 223 pp.

Cuisinier, Jeanne
1936 *Danse Magique de Kelantan*. Institut d'Ethnologie, XXII (University of Paris), 206 pp.

Farmer, George
1926 *A History of Arabian Music* (London: Luzac).

Jairazbhoy, Nazir
1970 "A Preliminary Survey of the Oboe in India," *Ethnomusicology*, Vol. XIV, no. 3, 375-388.

Jiwa, Tunku N., R. B. Shah, & H. M. Sheppard
1962 "The Kedah and Perak Nobat," Malaya in History, Vol. VII, no. 2, 7-11.

Kunst, Jaap
1949 Music in Java. (The Hague: Nijhoff), 2 vols.

Malm, William P.
1967 Music Cultures of the Pacific, the Near East, and Asia. (Englewood Cliffs, N.J.: Prentice-Hall), 169 pp.

1969 "Music of the Ma'yong," Tenggara, 5, 114-120.

1972 "On the Meaning and Invention of the Term Disphony," Ethnomusicology, Vol. XVI, no. 2 (May, 1972), 247-249.

Marcel-Dubois, Claudie
1941 Les Instruments de Musique de l'Inde Ancienne. (Paris: Université de France) 259 pp.

Marcuse, Sibyl
1964 Music Instruments: A Comprehensive Dictiona (New York: Doubleday & Co.), 608 pp.

Mohamed Taib Osman
1969 "Some Observations on the Socio-Cultural Context of Traditional Malay Music," Tenggara, 5, 121-128.

Sachs, Curt
1940 The History of Musical Instruments. (New York: Norton), 505 pp.

Sheppard, Tansri Dato Haji Mubin
1967 "Joget gamalan Trengganu," Journal of the Malaysian Branch, Royal Asiatic Society, Vol. XL, pt. 1, 149-152.

1969 "Ma'yong, The Malay Dance Drama," Tenggara, 5, 107-113.

1972 Taman Indera. (London: Oxford University Press), 207 pp.

Singaravelu, S.
1969 "Invocations to Nataraja in the Southeast Asian Shadow Plays," paper read at the International Conference on Traditional Drama and Music of Southeast Asia. Kuala Lumpur, August.

Sweeney, P. L. Amin
n.d. Malay Shadow Puppets: The Wayang Siam of Kelantan. (London: British Museum), 83 pp.

1972 The Ramayana and the Malay Shadow-Play. (Kuala Lumpur: National University of Malaysia Press), 464 pp.

Swettenham, Frank A.
1959 "A Malay Nautch," Malaya in History (Feb.) Vol. 5, no. 1, 38-41. Reprint of 1878 report.

Yupho, Dhanit
1960 Thai Musical Instruments. (Bangkok: Siva Phorn), Trans. by David Morton, 104 pp.

Zieseniss, Alexander
1963 The Rama Saga in Malaysia. (Singapore: Research Ltd.), 203 pp.

DISCOGRAPHY

Item 1 Folk and Ethnic Music of Malaysia. Radio Malaysia Recording RMT - 4

Item 2 The Music of Malaysia, Ma'yong Theatre Music of Kelantan. Anthology Records AST 4006

Item 3 The Music of Turkey (Mevlevi music). Anthology Records AST 4003

Item 4 Recitals from the Holy Koran. Parlophone LBVM 23

Item 5 Sufi Ceremony. Folkways FR 8942

Item 6 Temiar Dream Music. Folkways P 460

Item 7 Tuareg Music of the Southern Sahara. Folkways FE 4470

BOOK RECORD

This term refers to an LP recording of materials from the studies of this monograph plus those of the anthology of oral folk literature of Southeast Asia now in preparation.

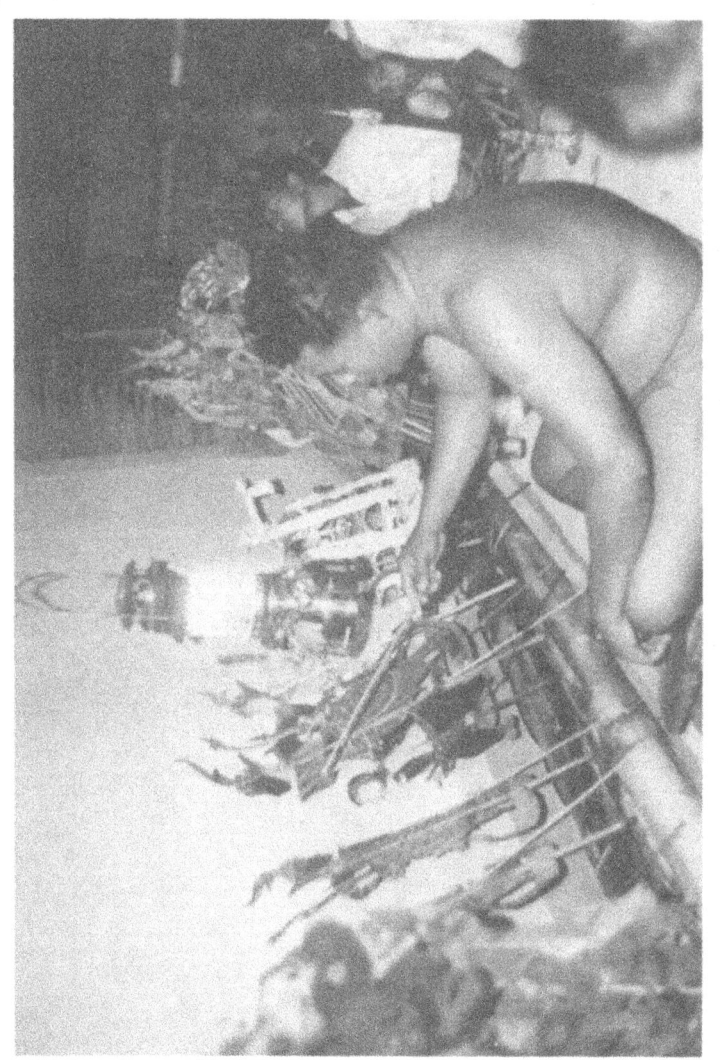

Plate I. Wayang Kulit (note the serunai).

Plate II. Gendang keling.

Plate III. Rebana ubi.

Plate IV. Ma'yong.

Plate V. The elephant in a Ma'yong.

Plate VI. A lupa dance in Putri.

EXAMPLE I

42

EXAMPLE 2

EXAMPLE 3

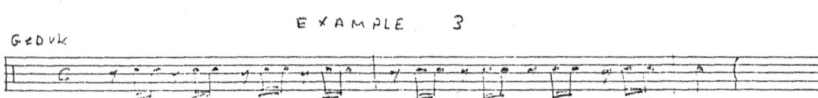

43

EXAMPLE 4

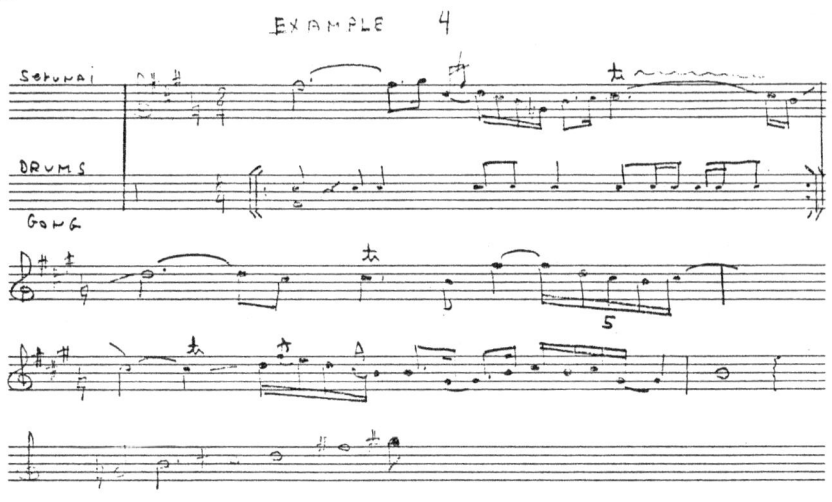

EXAMPLE 5

EXAMPLE 6

45

EXAMPLE 7

PROFESSIONAL MALAY STORY-TELLING

Some Questions of Style and Presentation

by

AMIN SWEENEY

Grateful acknowledgement is made to the Journal of the Malaysian Branch of the Royal Asiatic Society for their permission to reprint this article.

PROFESSIONAL MALAY STORY-TELLING
Some questions of style and presentation
by
Amin Sweeney

Preliminary Remarks

It is remarkable evidence of the almost sacred aura surrounding the printed word in Malay society that many literate Malays, when asked about the tales of Sang Kanchil or Pak Pandir, will refer the inquirer to the published texts of *Hikayat Sang Kanchil* (Dussek, 1915) and *Cherita Jenaka* (Winstedt, 1941), informing him that these are the 'standard' or 'correct' versions. It is forgotten that the books themselves originated from oral forms, collected over fifty years ago on the initiative of British administrators, and that these oral forms still continue to exist in Malay society.[1] For decades, courses on Malay literature in schools and universities have commenced with a number of lectures on 'Malay folk-literature', using such published texts as *Hikayat Awang Sulung Merah Muda* (Winstedt, 1957a), *Hikayat Malim Deman* (Winstedt, 1957b) and the two mentioned above. The methodology employed to study such texts has been identical to that used on literary works; and plot, language, style and imagery are discussed and evaluated.

All this has little to do with *oral* literature, however. The texts of 'folk literature' published during the last ninety odd years have all been put into literary Malay and are, in varying degrees, to be regarded more as the work of the scribe than of the teller. Thus, for example, if we were to remark that the *Cherita Pak Pandir* (Winstedt, 1941) works up to a climax with the killing of the ogre, we would, in fact, merely be commenting on the abilities of the compiler, for it is he who joined together a large number of episodes which, in oral tradition, are distinct stories.[2] The screen interposed between the teller and ourselves by the interpretation and remoulding of a third party, the writer, has resulted in our losing sight of the *oral* nature of oral literature and, although every member of Malay society is the bearer of a variety of oral tradition, he often fails to recognize it as such.

In view of the hitherto almost exclusive concern with content, it is my intention in this paper to attempt to throw some light upon the form, style and presentation of oral Malay literature, with special reference to that class of story-telling popularly known as *penglipur lara*, or what Winstedt termed 'folk romances'. The stories of this type, collected at the end of the nineteenth and beginning of the twentieth centuries by colonial officers such as Maxwell, Clifford, Sturrock and Winstedt have,

---

[1] A forthcoming paper, "The Pak Pandir Cycle of Tales," will examine this question.
[2] And it should be remembered that any evaluation of the compiler's work must be preceded by an examination of the norms and criteria of his time, which are not those of today.

in common with other genres of folk literature, all been adapted into literary Malay; the editors have presented little information on the original form, and what is provided is vague and, in cases, contradictory. The actual work of adapting these tales was apparently always done by Malay scribes such as Raja Haji Yahya bin Raja Mat Ali, and the texts, as they stand, differ only from palace *hikayat* literature in that they contain examples of 'rhythmical prose'.[3]

This, however, is not a matter for criticism. The main aim of the editors of these works was to provide suitable reading material for vernacular schools, and the adaptors would naturally, and quite rightly so, discard the conventions of oral literature and employ literary style for a written medium. The adaptation of tales from an oral to a literary medium, moreover, was practised long before the efforts of the British, as is apparent from the existence of literary works such as *Hikayat Pelanduk Jenaka* (Klinkert 1893, Dussek, 1915) and a variety of *wayang* tales clearly oral in origin. More recently, the *Dewan Bahasa dan Pustaka* and such indefatigable amateurs as Zakaria bin Hitam[4] have produced a number of *penglipur lara* tales, all of which have, in varying degrees, been presented in easily understood literary prose. The *Dewan Bahasa* is a commercial enterprise and each publication must be a viable proposition. Here again, however, it is to be regretted that, with few exceptions,[5] the editors make little mention of the original form. The whole question of adaptation from an oral to a literary medium makes an interesting field of study and I shall endeavour, in passing, to reveal some of the methods employed by the adaptors of *penglipur lara* tales.

Stylized and non-stylized form

The differences between the language of everyday conversation and literary style are considerable in any society. When writing, we tend to lavish far more attention on grammar and style than when communicating in informal conversation, where our words, once uttered, cease to exist. Also, when speaking in public, which requires a formal manner, we are likely to employ a literary style and may well prepare and write down our words beforehand. The language we use thus varies between casual everyday conversation and non-casual literary style, depending upon the context.

In traditional Malay society, before the days of mass education, the great majority of the population were illiterate, and penmanship was an exclusive art. Writers were professionals, combining, as Skinner (1963: 27) has pointed out, the tasks of artist and craftsman. In such a society, literary style was bound by many conventions, in keeping with its exclusive nature. The reading public in this age of manuscript

---

[3] And even this is found in some early or unsophisticated palace literature, e.g. *Hikayat Raja-raja Pasai* (Hill, 1960) and *Salasilah Kutai* (Mees, 1935). Some of the folk romances still contain traces of the '*kampung* world view,' however.

[4] An Academic Exercise of the University of Malaya has been written concerning the materials collected by Encik Zakaria (Yaakub bin Isa, 1971).

[5] Two exceptions are *Selindung Bulan Kedah Tua* (Awang Had, 1964) and *Si Suton* (Hamsiah, 1964b), which contain some brief remarks on the presentation.

literature and widespread illiteracy was limited, but *hikayat* and *sha'ir* were read aloud to audiences, so that society was often well-acquainted with the content of such works.

It should not, however, be thought that oral Malay literature was (or is) limited to the language of everyday conversation. Just as the language of written literature is a stylized form of everyday speech, regulated by various conventions, similarly in the pre-literate or semi-literate areas of Malay society, we find that oral tradition has developed stylized forms of language and presentation, which also differ considerably from those of everyday speech. This stylized oral form, as regards language, is best seen in the most developed genres of oral literature, such as *wayang kulit* and *Mak Yong*, where the use of distortions of grammar and pronunciation, special *wayang* words and phrases, and various other devices, results in a 'heightened' form of the local dialect (see further Sweeney, 1972: 63–72). However, in speaking of stylized form, we cannot confine our remarks to the style of the language in isolation; a presentation of oral narrative literature in stylized form is not just a recital but will, depending upon the genre in question, employ other media of communication such as singing, musical accompaniment and drama which, from our modern viewpoint, constitute separate art forms, but which, in oral Malay tradition, are fused together in the totality of the art. In this paper, therefore, the term 'non-stylized oral form' is used to describe the language and gesture of everyday conversation, while 'stylized oral form' refers to that mode of expression where the language employed and its presentation are not those of normal speech.

Furthermore, just as penmanship was at one time almost entirely in the hands of professionals, so we find that the exponents of stylized oral narrative, too, are usually professionals,[6] and the reverse is certainly the case, i.e. a professional performance is always in stylized form. This is hardly surprising: a businessman must be able to provide a commodity which his potential customers do not already possess. Yet every member of Malay society is a bearer of oral tradition, and the great majority are active bearers in varying degrees, but, in the case of narrative, the medium will usually be the language of everyday speech. The professional performer must therefore present his wares in a saleable form.

---

[6] While we are only concerned with oral narrative in this paper, it may be noted that in non-narrative oral literature, too, the exponents of stylized form are often professionals as, for example, in the field of traditional medicine and spirit mediumship. There are, of course, exceptions, e.g. *pantun*, songs and lullabies, proverbs, camphor language etc. And even in the case of oral narrative there are exceptions as, for example, the *dalang tiru* and *dalang budak* of the *wayang Siam* (Sweeney, 1972: 41). And, as regards *penglipur lara*, in those genres where the technique is relatively simple, as in Pahang, it is not unknown for individuals to have picked up stories in stylized form but never to have performed them professionally. Such a person might recite snatches of his stories in stylized form, but I have never heard of a full stylized performance being presented by an amateur. [While professional story-tellers may perform at marriages and circumcisions, performances are by no means restricted to such occasions, and may be held at any time (except perhaps during *Ramadhan*)].

The different modes of expression may be shown on a triangular figure, where,

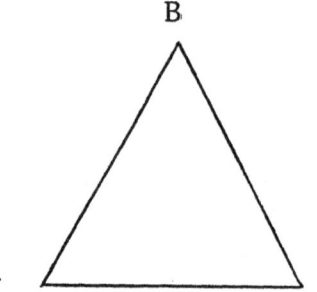

A = oral, non-stylized, amateur, informal.
B = literary, stylized, (formerly) professional, formal.
C = oral, stylized, professional, formal.

The types of narrative literature presented in these categories are not mutually exclusive and a wide variety of adaptation is possible between A, B and C: literary stories are retold in everyday speech (B → A); they are also adapted to the stylized oral form, thus, for example, written Panji tales are presented in the *wayang Jawa* (B → C). Stories in stylized oral form may be recounted in everyday speech (C → A) or may be turned into literary works as, for example, *Selindung Bulan Kedah Tua* (Awang Had, 1964) (C → B). Non-stylized tales may be written down, as in the *Cherita Jenaka* (A → B) or many be turned into stylized renderings, as in the case of *dalangs*, who often adapt simple stories for presentation (A → C). As regards points A & C, however, there are certain classes of story which are usually told only in the non-stylized form as, for example, Pak Pandir and mousedeer stories. Even when told by a professional storyteller, they will be in everyday speech. He will not tell them '*ex officio*' and they do not form part of his marketable stock-in-trade.[7] More will be said regarding the narration of these amateur stories in the forthcoming paper referred to above.

The points of the triangle ABC do not, however, represent self-contained and independent categories, and each of the sides of the figure may be regarded as a continuum. Here we shall mention only A:C. For example, as I have demonstrated previously (Sweeney, 1972: 49–53), a *dalang* may recount his repertoire in narrative form, without the aid of puppets or music, for the benefit of a pupil. He will tend to veer between two modes of narration, casual or non-casual, depending on the social context. The less casual his approach, the more closely his speech resembles that of a *wayang* performance; and the more casual it is, the more his speech becomes that of everyday conversation. Similarly, the non-*dalang* professional story-teller, when 'off-duty', may recount his story in simple narrative, which will be casual or non-casual, again depending on the context. In the latter case, although his narration will mainly be in everyday speech, he may include passages of so-called 'rhythmical prose'. In the same way, members of his audience will often be able to retell the tales in everyday language and may well include snatches of stylized language they have remembered.

The apparently contradictory information provided by collectors, concerning the presentation of *penglipur lara* tales, has resulted from a failure on their part to take into account these considerations. Thus, Maxwell (1886: 87) speaks of the story-

---

[7] And here the exception proves the rule: when Mahmud (Perlis) recently performed in Kuala Lumpur, he presented the story of *Pak Kaduk* in stylized form, and this was considered a great joke by Mahmud and other professional performers who were present.

teller "intoning the words in a monotonous chant as if he were reading aloud from a book." On the other hand, Winstedt (1957a: 149) tells us that "the prose parts of a Malay folk-tale are told by the rhapsodist in the language of conversation," and (1957b: flyleaf) speaks of "shapeless colloquial passages." Both Maxwell and Winstedt lay stress on the fact that the tales were taken down 'verbatim' from the lips of the reciter, and in this lies the key to the problem: no story-teller could perform in stylized form at dictation speed; and no transcriber could hope to keep up with and record faithfully the language of a typical stylized rendering, even though this be Maxwell's 'native writers' using *jawi* script, not to mention Europeans such as Winstedt, who also claims to have transcribed stories 'verbatim'. Winstedt was, therefore, no doubt correct in speaking of 'the language of conversation'; it is only unfortunate that he omitted to mention or was not aware that such renderings were, apart from the inclusion of rhythmical prose, recounted in the non-stylized form. Thus, it is clear that Malay writers, such as Raja Haji Yahya, did not adapt their works into literary form from the 'monotonous chant' of the stylized form, but worked from the 'colloquial passages' of the non-stylized form. And when later scholars, such as J. C. Bottoms, (1963: 6), expressed a desire to know "to what extent the end result is different from the original .... We *want* those 'shapeless colloquial passages' which are said to have been tidied; and we want them in their original form," they would, even if this wish were granted, still have gained little insight into the *penglipur lara* as an artistic form.[8]

In recent years the *Dewan Bahasa dan Pustaka* has published a number of *penglipur lara* texts. The introductions to all but two of these works tell us nothing about the stylized form. For example, in the introduction to *Bongsu Pinang Peribut* (Hamsiah, 1964a), we are told that, in general, *penglipur lara* tales from Pahang are presented in ordinary prose. And indeed, when the tapes are consulted, these tales are found to be rendered in the non-stylized form, apart from some passages of rhythmical prose. The concern of the editors to preserve as much as possible of the original in their texts,[9] therefore, while admirable from the point of view of preserving the *content*, will not, however, enable us to appreciate the artistic performance of the *penglipur lara*.

Here again we see that collectors and editors did not take into account the existence of, nor attempt to distinguish between, stylized and non-stylized forms. The Pahang tales published by the *Dewan Bahasa dan Pustaka* are *Bongsu Pinang Peribut* (Hamsiah, 1964a), *Raja Donan* (Zaharah Khalid, 1963) and *Raja Gagak* (Zaharah Taha, 1963). My examination of the reciters, respectively Ahmad bin Hood, Esah binti Mat Akil and Jidin bin Ali, revealed this distinction: Jidin and

---

[8] Bottoms himself apparently did not distinguish between stylized and non-stylized, for, although he notes that stories are sung, he recorded them all in the non-stylized form (Bottoms, 1963: 20).

[9] With regard to language, the editors attempted to achieve two conflicting aims: to adapt the tale into literary prose and yet at the same time to preserve the language of the original, (i.e. the unstylized form of the teller). This, of course, is impossible and resulted in such linguistic mortal sins as 'Yang saya ubah dalam penulisan cherita ini ialah perkataan-perkataan yang, pada hemat saya, salah tata-bahasanya." (Zaharah Taha 1963, viii).

Esah, in the proper social context,[10] present their stories in stylized form; both are professional story-tellers. Ahmad Hood is an amateur, presenting his tale only in the non-stylized form, which is a non-marketable commodity.[11]

Genres of Professional Story-telling

At this point we may proceed to examine the *penglipur lara* in some detail. The materials for this study were gathered intermittently over a period extending from 1968 to 1973. The earlier part of the work concentrated mainly on the *tarik selampit* of Kelantan. The second phase of the study included a survey of the states of West Malaysia and Patani in Southern Thailand. In this task I received the full co-operation of the *Dewan Bahasa dan Pustaka* who generously allowed me to consult their collection of tapes and inventory of narrators from which I was able to trace a number of story-tellers previously recorded by the *Dewan*. Information from my students also enabled me to contact several others and to establish that no performers were to be found in certain areas. A large part of the task, however, involved travelling from village to village and making inquiries 'on the ground'.

Almost every member of Malay society is able to recount, at least when pressed, short animal, farcical and origin tales etc., but few can relate longer stories of the 'folk-romance' type. Of the latter, the majority narrate the tale in the language of everyday conversation and expect no reward for their trouble from the members of their own society. A number of narrators, however, in the proper social context, will relate their tales in stylized form, and for this task they will receive a fee of some kind. A more detailed study was made of a representative sample of the latter,[12] the results of which appear in this paper. Field methods used were largely similar to those employed in my study of the shadow-play (Sweeney, 1972: 8–11). Recordings were made of the same story-teller performing the same story on different occasions, to assess the degree of variation. In some cases this involved recording the whole story; in others only samples were collected. Some story-tellers were recorded twice within a matter of days and then again a year later. One Kelantan performer was recorded four times over a period of four years.

A popular term for folk romances and their narrators is *penglipur lara*. As far as I am aware, the term, used specifically of oral story-tellers, first appeared in print in 1886 (Maxwell, 1886:87). However, none of the performers examined in this study referred to themselves, or were referred to, by this title. In Kelantan, Patani, Perlis and Kedah, the various genres of story-telling and their performers are usually known by the name of the hero of the most popular story in the repertoire of each genre. Thus, in Kelantan-Patani we find the *Tok Selampit* who performs the *tarik Selampit*, Selampit being the hero of the tale of the same name. Similarly, in Perlis and Langkawi there is the *Awang Batil* or *Awang Belanga*, and the *Selampit* (a different

---

[10] See note 16. The recording sessions of the *Dewan Bahasa* were obviously not 'traditional' occasions.

[11] He has adapted the tale into *sha'ir* form and in his story-telling he veers between non-stylized and literary style.

[12] The very limited number of story-tellers encountered meant that selection was unnecessary in most areas, with the exception of Pahang.

genre and tale from that of Kelantan); in Kedah there is the *Tok Jubang*, who performs the tale *Jubang Linggang*. I did not encounter this practice in Pahang where, apparently, story-tellers are simply referred to as *ahli cherita*. Isahak, a Perlis story-teller of the *Selampit* type, also referred to himself by this term. The various genres studied are distinguished in the figure below:—

genre	area	presentation	music
Tarik Selampit	Kelantan Patani Perlis [only one perfomer, a Kelantanese].	singing chanting speech	rebab
Selampit	Perlis Langkawi	chanting	*gendang Keling* or none
Awang Batil	Perlis Langkawi	chanting *or* rhythmic speech	*batil*
Jubang	Kedah [the two performers are of Patani extraction]	singing *or* chanting	none
Ahli cherita (no specific name)	Pahang Trengganu	singing *or* chanting	*rebana* or none
Kaba	Selangor [only one performer, an immigrant from Sumatra]	chanting	violin [properly, a *rebab*.]

Fig. 2.

I make no claim to have met or even to have traced all the performers of *penglipur lara* in stylized form. Nevertheless, I believe it possible to provide at least a rough estimate of their numbers and distribution. In Perlis I interviewed four performers (2 *Selampit* type, 1 *Awang Batil*, and 1 *tarik Selampit* whose performer is a Kelantanese who settled in Perlis many years ago), and heard of no others still alive. In Kedah proper only two could be traced (both *Tok Jubang* of Patani extraction) but two others are to be found in Langkawi (one *Selampit* and one *Awang Batil*).[13] According to information provided by many persons in Kedah, both *Selampit* and *Awang Batil* were previously also found in Kedah proper. Today, however, they only survive in the periphery of the area. Only one performer was traced in Patani *(tarik Selampit)* and four in Kelantan (also *tarik Selampit*). In Pahang I interviewed three performers but am aware of the existence of at least five others in Pahang and four

---

[13] I am most grateful to Datuk Syed Idrus al-Idrus of Alor Setar for allowing me to consult his recordings of these Langkawi performers.

in up-river Trengganu who perform a similar type. I suspect there are more, but bad communications and the fact that reputations only extend to a few surrounding villages make the task of tracing performers a formidable one.[14] There is also one performer in Selangor, but he is a Minangkabau immigrant, resident here for the past 35 years, who recites *kaba* mainly for Minangkabau speakers.[15] I did not succeed in tracing any performers in the other states of West Malaysia.

Professional status

By 'professional story-teller', we mean a performer who, in the traditional context,[16] is formally invited to perform at a specified place and time, and expects to be rewarded for his trouble. This definition of professional status thus includes not merely performers who derive a major part of their incomes from their art, but extends also to those who may perform perhaps only once in five years and are content with a 'small reward, a hearty welcome and a good meal'.

The elite of story-tellers are to be found in Perlis. Two well-known performers are Ismail bin Hasan, an exponent of *Selampit*, and Mahmud bin Wahid, who performs *Awang Batil*. Both apparently derive an important part of their incomes from performing. Ismail expects to be paid M$ 25 for a five-hour performance, in which he chants the stories of *Selampit* or *Si Suton*, usually without any accompaniment. On request, however, he will include his *gendang Keling*. This is a four-man orchestra, consisting of a *serunai* (oboe), two *gendang* (hand drums), and a pair of gongs. The *gendang Keling*, while not actually accompanying the performer's recital, is used to provide opening music and to illustrate various performances described in the story. Thus, for example, when the narrator describes a *wayang kulit* at the ruler's court, he stops chanting and, accompanied by the *gendang Keling*, simulates a *wayang kulit* performance for several minutes. In the absence of the orchestra, he will make do with drumming on his thighs.

Mahmud, the exponent of *Awang Batil*, recites his story and accompanies himself on a *batil* (brass bowl). He also makes use of masks during his performance, which are of the type used in the Kedah *Mak Yong*, one being a mask of the *hulubalang* (a captain, who is sent to summon people,) the other of the *nujum* (astrologer). When

---

[14] Although many stories have been collected by Zakaria Hitam (see note 4), as far as I am aware, no distinction has been made between stylized/non-stylized.

[15] He is atypical in that he learnt his stories from the published *kaba* texts, and is not included in this study.

[16] I have emphasized the matter of traditional context for two reasons: research workers are accustomed to pay their informants a fee regardless of whether the latter are amateurs or professionals in their own *milieu;* secondly, in view of the fact that a recording session is not a traditional occasion for a performance, the onus is upon the research worker to create the atmosphere required for a typical performance. When recording amateurs, he must put the informant at his ease by creating the informal atmosphere in which the story would normally be told to friends and relatives, and, indeed, an audience should be present. When a professional is to be recorded, the research worker must again be able to create the correct conditions in which such a presentation would normally be given. If this is not done, the informant, faced with a stranger armed with a tape-recorder, may not be able to relate the situation to his own pattern of experience; in such cases he may decide that a stranger would not understand the stylized form or, again, if the context is too informal, he may feel the occasion merits the non-stylized form that he would use in 'off-duty' narrations.

either of these characters appears in the story, Mahmud dons the relevant mask and continues his narrative thus attired while describing the actions and voicing the words of the *hulubalang* or *nujum*. Thus, although the form is still narrative, a dramatic element is introduced. For a night's performance Mahmud expects to receive at least M$10, the fee being in theory $12.15.

Ismail claims to receive about thirty invitations a year to perform *Selampit*. Mahmud considerably more, but Ismail's fewer performances are compensated for by his higher fee. These two performers derive a major share of their income from their art. This is not, however, the case with all story-tellers in the area. Haji Isahak bin Daud, now 85 years of age and no longer performing, is a reciter of the *Selampit* type but his story-telling seems to have been more of a sideline rather than a primary occupation. This also appears to be the case with the two story-tellers on Langkawi.

While the *Tok Selampit* of Kelantan-Patani is well able to compete with the story-tellers of Perlis in terms of skill and technique, he lags a long way behind, at least nowadays, in popularity. In the *tarik Selampit*, the performer sings, chants and speaks, accompanying himself on a three-stringed *rebab* (spike fiddle). When characters in the story engage in dialogue, the narrator will often omit indications of who is speaking, such as 'X said' or 'Y answered', so that such pieces assume the form of drama. There is no fixed rate of fee and a performer would be fortunate to receive M$10 nightly. Usually he will only get $4 or $5 or even less. The *tarik Selampit* is no longer popular in Kelantan or Patani, and Mat Nor, the most active performer, is lucky if he receives as many as ten (one night)[17] invitations to perform in a year. Thus, the *Tok Selampit* of Kelantan-Patani today derives only a very insignificant part of his income from his art. The poor attendance at performances of *tarik Selampit* is clear evidence of the lack of interest in this genre today: on several occasions I have held performances, given by well-known reciters, at my house in Kota Baru; an audience of perhaps twenty people would assemble, but after about an hour they would gradually drift away, usually to watch the television next door. Even in rural areas such as Bachok, the heart of *tarik Selampit* country, attendance at performances is only marginally better. This lack of interest is attributed locally to the competition from *wayang kulit*, *dikir barat*, films and television. Although it is true that these other entertainments are currently very popular, the *tarik Selampit* has always been overshadowed by more sophisticated traditional arts such as *wayang kulit* and *Mak Yong*, and the main culprit appears to be television.

In the other areas of West Malaysia, i.e. the Sik-Baling districts of Kedah, Pahang and the up-river parts of Trengganu, professional story-telling is a much more modest affair. Tales are sung or chanted, usually without any accompaniment, although in Pahang a *rebana* is sometimes used. Nowadays performances are quite rare, and a reciter may find that five years go by without a single invitation to perform. Income from story-telling in these areas is thus, in general, negligible. Although it seems almost certain that performances were far more frequent in the past, I found

---

[17] The majority of performances in all areas appear to be one-night affairs, at least nowadays, but there is no limit in theory.

no evidence to indicate that the exponents ever derived a major share of their incomes from the art.

Indeed, it is clear that there is a direct relationship between the complexity of the art and the performer's professional status. Thus, in the case of Ismail and Mahmud of Perlis, whose performances are quite elaborate, the art constitutes their major occupation, whereas in Pahang, where the presentation is very modest, it does not. However, some qualification is necessary here.

Firstly, we are not concerned with whether story-telling actually provides the major part of the performer's income at the present time, for this is determined by the frequency of invitations, and lack of interest in Kelantan, for example, ensures that *tarik Selampit* is the secondary occupation of the performer. What is important is whether the art is *intended* to earn a major part of his income. Thus, for example, the application necessary to master the arts of Kelantan *Selampit* singing, chanting and *rebab* playing, not to mention the financial outlay needed to buy the *rebab*, ensured that only those intending to make the art their profession would embark on learning to perform. By contrast, in areas such as Pahang, where presentation of stories is relatively simple, the potential performer is faced with a much less exacting task, and none of the story-tellers interviewed in Pahang seems to have expected that his art would earn him a major means of livelihood.

Secondly, in speaking of presentation, we have remarked on the complexity of certain performances in Perlis and Kelantan. Here, however, we must make a distinction between basic technique and elaboration. In Kelantan it is the basic technique which is complex, and any aspiring performer must first master this technique. In the case of the Perlis *Selampit* and *Awang Batil*, however, the basic technique is relatively simple. This is then elaborated by performers who intend to make the art their major occupation. Thus, the simple basic technique is seen in the performances of reciters such as Haji Isahak, whose presentation is on a very modest scale, comparable to that of Pahang story-tellers, and for whom performing is only a sideline. In the hands of showmen such as Ismail, however, this presentation becomes a good deal more elaborate, with the introduction of a dramatic element and the use of the *gendang Keling*. Similarly, the introduction of masks into the *Awang Batil* results in a much more sophisticated presentation.

We have seen that there are widely varying degrees of professional status. In no case, however, is story-telling the performer's only source of income. It may be said of traditional Malay entertainments in general that the exponents only very rarely attempt to subsist entirely on their incomes from performing, and even the most popular *dalangs* of the *Wayang Siam*, who may be invited to perform almost the whole year round, will nearly always have a secondary occupation. This is usually small-scale agricultural work, for almost all performers of traditional drama and story-telling are rural people, and the majority are illiterate or semi-illiterate. Indeed the rate of illiteracy among story-tellers is higher than in other genres, for a not inconsiderable number of performers are blind, especially in Kelantan where *tarik Selampit* is traditionally a profession for blind people. At the present, only in Perlis does story-telling constitute the primary occupation of performers and even there, only in the case of Ismail and Mahmud. Elsewhere it is story-telling which becomes the secondary occupation, at least in terms of the income derived. A number of story-tellers are also professional performers of other arts. Thus, Ismail (Perlis) is a teacher of *silat;* Mahmud (Perlis) also plays the *serunai* in the *gendang Keling;* Mat Nor (Kelantan) earns a dollar or two playing his *rebab* at *puteri* seances (spirit mediumship). Nevertheless, the total earnings from performing are never enough to provide a satisfactory livelihood. The more fortunate of story-tellers have their own patches of land which they or their families will tend. Even so, their economic lot is rarely any better than that of their fellow peasants. Where a story-teller has no land, as in the case of Mahmud and Mat Nor, and no regular secondary occupation, apart from perhaps hiring out his labour during the padi harvest, he faces a very meagre existence. A further handicap for many story-tellers, especially in Kelantan, is that they are blind or otherwise physically disabled. Where an individual has some other marketable skill and many solicitous relatives, as in the case of Jidin, an expert fish-trap maker, he may enjoy a satisfactory standard of living. When however, as in several instances in Kelantan, a blind story-teller has equipped himself for life only with his art, he may live a poverty-stricken existence. Thus, Mat Nor, apart from his meagre income from the *tarik Selampit*, is forced to rely on what his wife can earn harvesting padi and weaving mats, which is seldom much. Possessing no land, a major part of their diet comes from the few fish Mat Nor can catch and the vegetables they plant around their hut. And Setapa, the oldest *Tok Selampit* in Kelantan and Mat Nor's teacher, is reduced to begging for his other occupation, although in his case he is cared for by his family, and the begging seems to be more of a hobby!

Performer's Mystique

A further aspect of professional story-telling is a number of practices, attitudes, assumptions and beliefs which surround the performer and his art with a certain mystique and set him apart from the common man. This 'performer's mystique' will be discussed under a number of headings which, taken collectively, serve as a fair guide to a performer's professionalism.

A number of story-tellers attach considerable importance to legitimacy. This may be attained either by heredity or by having a teacher. Enquiry revealed that, in most cases, story-tellers are fairly evenly distributed between those who acquired their art from parents or relatives, and those who learnt from persons unrelated to them. Only three performers (Awang Lah in Patani, Ismail in Perlis, and Abdullah Omar in Kedah) claim to have acquired their art from their fathers. In Kelantan, however, the *Tok Selampit* rarely learns from his parents, or even relatives. This appears to be due to the fact that *tarik Selampit* is traditionally a profession for the blind.[18] This blindness, however, is generally caused by vitamin A deficiency and is not hereditary, so that it is unlikely that a *selampit's* father or offspring would also perform *tarik Selampit*. Furthermore, the fact of blindness itself tends to militate against an individual's chances of raising a family. Outside Kelantan, however,

---

[18] But by no means exclusively so; see page 61.

in Perlis and Patani, I encountered two exponents of *tarik Selampit* who were not blind, and it is interesting to note that both of them claim to have inherited their art.

Here, however, we are not so much concerned with the relationship of the story-teller to the person from whom he acquired his art, as with the degree of importance which he himself attaches to this relationship as a source of legitimacy. Thus, Ismail of Perlis and Awang Lah of Patani lay great stress on heredity *(menanggung pesaka)*. Isahak (Perlis) is obviously proud that he acquired his stories from his uncle, the well-known Panglima Ali Hassan,[19] and he, too, views this in the context of *menanggung pesaka*. By contrast, very little importance is attached to heredity by the story-tellers interviewed in Kedah and Pahang. Thus, although Abdullah Omar (Kedah) acquired his tales from his father; Esah (Pahang) from her grandfather, and Jidin (Pahang) from his aunt, none of them regards him/herself as 'inheriting' the art, nor is heredity seen as in any way enhancing their role as story-tellers. In Kelantan, too, it is not an important factor, although, as we have seen, a Kelantanese performer of the *tarik Selampit* in Perlis, Awang bin Abdullah, speaks of heredity, claiming to have received the art from his grandfather. The importance which he attaches to this, however, may reflect the attitudes of the Perlis society in which he has apparently lived for over fifty years. Similarly, in Patani, more prestige seems to be attached to heredity than in Kelantan, not only in *tarik Selampit*, but also in the *wayang Jawa* and *Mak Yong* where, in Kelantan, having a famous teacher is more important.

In the matter of having a teacher, i.e. one unrelated to the pupil, Mahmud (Perlis) lays considerable stress on the fact that he had a *guru* and speaks scathingly of those who merely 'picked up' the art. In Kelantan and Kedah (Had bin Mat Arif), mention is made of having a teacher, but far less importance is attached to the matter than in the case of Mahmud, as will become apparent below. And in Pahang, Hasan, who acquired his stories from an old story-teller who lived with Hasan's family, does not even speak of having a teacher, but merely says that he picked up the stories.

In actual fact, the method of acquiring stories would seem to be everywhere basically much the same. The simplest explanation of the process came from the Pahang storytellers. Thus, in the words of Hasan, "I used to hear him performing, over and over again. In the end the stories stuck *(lama-lama lekat)*." At the other end of the scale, in Perlis, however, the process of acquiring the art is surrounded by varying degrees of mystique. Thus, Ismail claimed to have had a dream in which an old man, clothed all in white, appeared to him and granted him the power to perform. He did not 'learn' the art nor will he teach it. When he stops performing, his successor, who he expects will be his nephew, will receive the art in similar fashion.[20] Ismail agreed, however, that he had heard his predecessor perform on

---

[19] The 'owner' of Winstedt's version of *Terung Pipit*, Panglima Ali Mudin bin Panglima Hasan (Winstedt, 1927).

[20] This is a useful mechanism to avoid rivalry from pupils, a constant bane of some Kelantanese *dalangs*. In Perlis, with its small population, one *Selampit* performer is sufficient to supply the demand for performances.

Plate 1. A Kelantan *Tok Selampit*, Mat Nor of Bachok, performing with his *rebab*.
(Photo Muzium Negara)

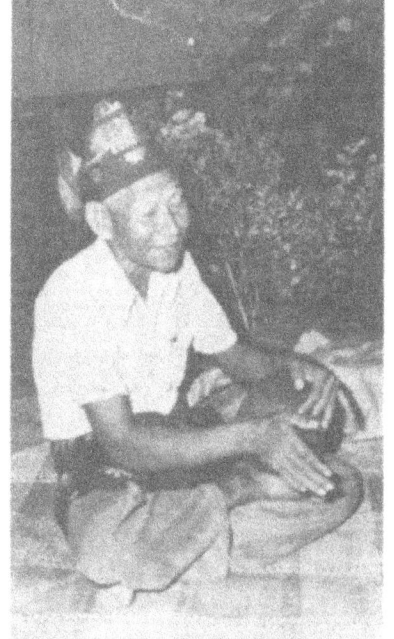

Plate 2. A Perlis *Awang Batil*, Mahmud bin Wahid of Kampong Mata Ayer.
(Photo Muzium Negara)

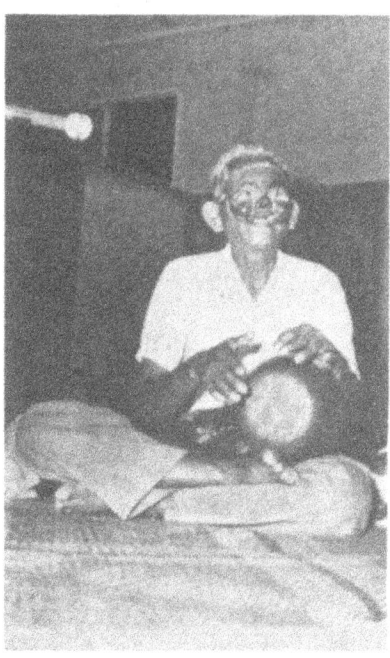

Plate 3. Mahmud of Perlis wearing his *hulubalang* mask.
(Photo Muzium Negara)

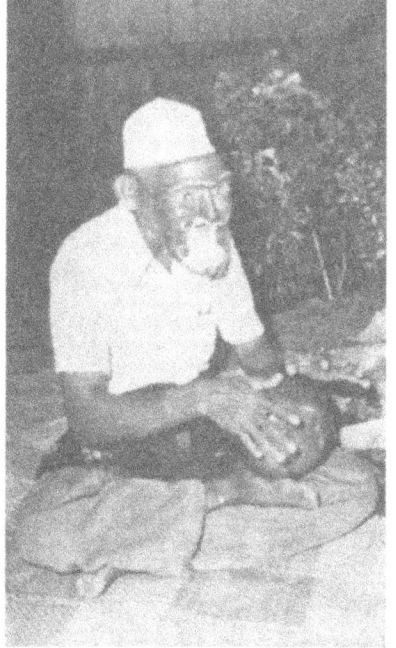

Plate 4. Mahmud of Perlis wearing his *nujum* mask.
(Photo Muzium Negara)

many occasions. Similarly, Awang Abdullah declared that he did not 'learn' but that the stories had 'come down' to him.

In the case of those story-tellers claiming to have learnt from a teacher, the method again seems to have been listening and imitating.[21] Some performers in this category appear to have had little if any formal instruction, and Mat Nor (Kelantan) recalls that he acquired his art mainly by listening to Setapa at regular performances and then imitating him. Mahmud (Perlis) and Had (Kedah), however, claim to have had formal training, and here, the method seems to have been demonstration and imitation, followed by criticism where necessary, but with little attention paid to theoretical instruction. But, as in the case of those who inherited their art, here, too, the process of learning to perform may be surrounded by mystique. Thus, according to Mahmud (Perlis) (but not, as far as I am aware, in other areas), the commencement and completion of the period of study must be ritually formalized by ceremonies of enrolment and graduation which, although on a much more modest scale (and not including trance), perform similar functions to the *peturun* and *pelimau* of the *Wayang Siam* (Sweeney, 1972: 43, 48).

A ritual more commonly found among story-tellers is the opening ceremony which precedes a performance and which, although again of much more modest proportions, performs a similar function to the *kenduri* of the *wayang kulit* and *Mak Yong* (Sweeney, 1972: 274). Thus, Mahmud and Ismail of Perlis, Had of Kedah and all the exponents of *tarik Selampit* interviewed commence performances with a simple ceremony, the common elements of which are the preparation of a dish of offerings, usually consisting of betel leaf and areca nut etc. and sometimes including a small amount of money, known as a *pekeras*;[22] the burning of incense *(kemenyan)* and a muttered invocation, usually inaudible. Of all the story-tellers interviewed, Ismail (Perlis) attaches the most importance to this ceremony, and declares himself incapable of reciting even a short passage of his stories unless he has first complied with the ritual requirements. He stresses that, in his normal state, he is unable to remember the details of a story, and that, during his opening ceremony, he must first make a request that the story or section of story he wishes to perform may be made available to him. Thus, he places his burning incense before him and passes his betel receptacle through the smoke, muttering inaudibly. He prepares a quid and commences to chew it. He then immerses his face and arms in the smoke, rubs it over his face, arms and back three times and pats himself on the back. He is now ready: his eyes are closed and, with an expression of intense concentration, he begins to intone his chant. Ismail stresses that not only must he never omit this ritual; he must also perform it correctly, otherwise he suffers a complete loss of appetite. With most story-tellers, an opening ceremony is held to ensure harmony during the

---

[21] None of the story-tellers interviewed had pupils, so I was denied the opportunity of observing teaching methods first-hand. Mahmud, however, was optimistic that one of his young relatives would learn the art from him. It may be noted that almost all the performers I met were aged over fifty. (See excerpts).

[22] I.e. *pekeras semangat* (lit. hardener of the vital essence). This is also employed by *dalangs* and *bomohs*. In story-telling the amount varies; thus e.g. Mat Nor's (Kelantan) *pekeras* is $2.15, Ismail's (Perlis) is $5.25 (at least in theory). Mat Nor does not require a *pekeras* for all stories, only those where the recital may entail some danger from the unseen world, e.g. *Raja Budak* and *Raja Dera*.

performance and to avoid intrusions from the unseen world. For Ismail, however, the ritual has the added function of enabling him to attain a state of detachment approaching that of trance. At the other end of the scale, in Pahang, I encountered no opening ritual at all. Even in Perlis, not all performers consider such practices necessary and in the 'unelaborated' *Selampit* type of Isahak, no opening ceremony is found.

Apart from the opening ritual, a number of story-tellers perform a *tabik* (greeting). This is sung or chanted in the same style as the story to follow. It is the 'curtain-raiser' in which the performer addresses his audience, including the denizens of the unseen world. In a passage of fairly fixed form he welcomes the assembly and apologizes for any shortcomings. In the most elaborate form, that of Mahmud, he stresses the fact that he has a teacher and is no mere imitator, assures his audience that they will be enthralled, and generally gives a display of showmanship or, in Mahmud's own words, *tunjuk ek* (shows off his act). Apart from Mahmud, the other story-tellers encountered who perform a *tabik* are Ismail (Perlis), Had (Kedah) and, in very brief form, Abdullah Omar (Kedah) and Hasan (Pahang). The *tabik* does not appear to be a feature of the Kelantan *tarik Selampit* however.[23]

An interesting phenomenon observed in several genres of professional Malay story-telling is the performer's dependence on what we may term a 'catalyst'. This is often the musical instrument that the performer employs; thus, for the Kelantan *Tok Selampit* his *rebab*, and for the *Awang Batil* his *batil*. Only when the *rebab* is in his hands, or the *batil* is on his lap does the performer gain his inspiration. Mahmud, Setapa and Mat Nor declare that, without their instruments, they have difficulty in remembering the details of their stories, even though only to relate them in the language of everyday conversation without actually playing a note of music. For Ismail, his catalyst is not a musical instrument but incense. We noted above that, when performing, he achieves a state of detachment from his surroundings. According to him, this state can only be maintained throughout the performance by bathing his face continuously in the incense fumes. He himself refers jokingly to the incense as his 'battery'. If the battery runs flat he is unable to continue. Consequently there must be an attendant who constantly replenishes the supply of incense. I observed this need for a catalyst only in the cases of Ismail, Mahmud and the exponents of the *tarik Selampit*. Elsewhere no such requirement was found, even where, as with Jidin (Pahang) and his *rebana*, a musical instrument was employed. We see the same need for the catalyst in the *wayang kulit*, where dalangs declare that only when they are in front of their screen with the puppets in their hands does their *angin* come and they are able to perform (Sweeney, 1972: 52).

---

[23] Nevertheless, there is sometimes a closing formula in which the spirits are sent back *(hantar balik)*. It will be noticed that I usually refer only to the Kelantan *tarik Selampit*. This is because I am unable to generalize on the Patani form of this genre. I encountered only one reciter in Patani and his performance was extremely corrupt: he did not use a *rebab* but a Chinese-style bowed chordophone which, to make matters worse, had no strings! And his style of singing resembled more that of *dikir barat* than *Selampit*. I hasten to add that this is not merely my own evaluation but also that of elderly Patani people who witnessed the proceedings.

From our examination of this sample of story-tellers, we see that, in terms of professionalism and showmanship, Ismail the *Selampit* and Mahmud the *Awang Batil* of Perlis are without rivals, while, at the other end of the scale, the story-tellers of Pahang make little attempt at elaboration or showmanship, contenting themselves with an unpretentious presentation of their tales. Not all performers in Perlis exhibit the same degree of professionalism, however. Side by side with the showmen there are performers of the same genre whose presentation is on a much more modest scale. In the Kelantan *tarik Selampit*, the basic technique is a good deal more complex than that of the Perlis *Selampit* or *Awang Batil*. There is not, however, the same elaboration, and the degree of professionalism is considerably more uniform than in Perlis. It is hardly surprising that there is less emphasis on performer's mystique in the *tarik Selampit* than in the case of the showmen of Perlis: traditionally it has been a profession for those people suffering from blindness or other physical handicap who possess the *angin* (see Sweeney, 1972: 42) to be performers. Those individuals with *angin* who were not handicapped in this way would choose to become exponents of more sophisticated genres such as *wayang kulit* or *Mak Yong*, which have thus overshadowed the *tarik Selampit*. A good illustration of the lack of prestige attached to the role of *Selampit* in Kelantan is provided by Karim, a well-known *dalang* of the *wayang Siam*. He informed me that, before becoming a *dalang*, he had experienced considerable poverty and, at one stage, he became so desperate that he tried his hand at *tarik Selampit*. The first time he performed, however, one of the audience asked him, "What's wrong with you then?" This was enough for Karim, who immediately abandoned his new occupation! As he explained, it is often *expected* that a *Tok Selampit* will have some physical defect.

We see furthermore, that the most developed forms of story-telling, i.e. in Perlis and Kelantan, are found in areas where there is padi-growing on a large scale. The social organization, better communications and presence of a period of leisure time after the padi-harvest in these areas have favoured the development of such arts, whereas, in most areas of Pahang, such advantages are lacking. Thus, for example, Ismail and Mahmud are known and perform throughout Perlis and even in Kedah, and both of them reveal keen professional rivalry; Mat Nor and Setapa are well-known throughout the coastal plain of Kelantan. In Pahang, however, performers rarely perform far away from home, and reputations are never wide-spread: Esah and Hasan were unaware of each other's existence, even though they live only a few miles apart.

The Technique

1. Intonation and Delimitation of Utterance

The intonation and delimitation of stretches of utterance in professional story-telling are not those of normal speech; the tales are sung, chanted or recited, and the length of each utterance is geared to the phrase of the melody or the rhythm of the recitation. At this point, it is convenient to make a distinction between two basic techniques, which we may term the 'repetitive' and the 'varied'. In those genres which employ a repetitive technique, the performer sings or intones his story using only one basic pattern of melody, which he repeats over and over again for the duration of the performance. Most genres of Malay story-telling are presented thus and only the Kelantan-Patani *tarik Selampit* is noticeably different in this respect, for here, the performer sings, chants and employs the intonation of normal speech. Moreover, his singing and chanting are not so rigidly confined to one set pattern and he has far more scope for improvisation. For the sake of convenience, therefore, the technique of the *tarik Selampit* will be discussed in detail **in a separate** paper and we shall first concentrate on the repetitive or strophic technique.

In the case of stories which are sung, the basic melody is very short, consisting of only a few phrases.[24] Thus, in the *Cherita Burung Raja Gagak* of Jidin (Pahang), the melody is roughly as follows:—

Here we see there are three phrases, which correspond to the first three lines of each 'verse' of the story (see excerpt Ph. 1); the last note of the third phrase is repeated several times in a monotone and the corresponding words are therefore printed as a separate line.

According to Jidin, in common with the other Pahang story-tellers interviewed, each tale has its own individual tune, and, indeed, he employed a different tune for each of four tales: *Burung Raja Gagak*, *Burung Agut*, *Raja Muda* and *Bongsu Pinang Peribut*. For example, in Jidin's rendering of *Burung Agut*, the melody is as follows:—

---

[24] All the musical notation in this paper is the work of Encik Abdul Fattah (see final 'Note'.) As minor inconsistencies occur from verse to verse, the notation presented is that of the most typical rendering of each performer.

In this example, there are three phrases divided into seven sections, each of which corresponds to a line in excerpt Ph. 2. It may be noted that in both tales, Jidin sometimes missed out or repeated a section or even a phrase of the melody. From his comments afterwards, however, it seems that this was due to absent-mindedness rather than design, and there was no set pattern of omission or repetition in this instance.

Examples from *Burung Gagak* and *Burung Agut* were again recorded at a later date and the same tunes were employed as before. In Kedah, too, this distinction is found. The tunes employed by Had in his renderings of *Jubang Linggang* and *Raja Lotong* are very similar, as is clear from the following:—

Jubang Linggang

Raja Lotong

Even so, Had took pains to distinguish between the two versions of the melody, and subsequent re-recordings of the same examples reveal that the distinctions are consistently maintained in each performance. In the excerpt from *Raja Lotong* (Kd. 2), the two sections of the first phrase are printed as one line. The second phrase is repeated several times. The last two sections of the final phrase correspond to the last line. The fourth phrase and the first section of the final phrase correspond to the penultimate line. In *Jubang Linggang* (Kd. 3), the first thirteen notes of the initial phrase are printed as one line, for they are sometimes omitted.

However, although individual performers have a specific tune for each story, this does not mean that all performers of a particular tale will use the same tune. For example, in Hasan's rendering of *Burung Agut*, the melody employed is entirely different from that of Jidin performing the same story:—

In this example, each phrase corresponds to one line of Excerpt Ph. 3. Also, Jidin and Hasan use different melodies for performing the tale of *Raja Muda*.

In Kedah, too, Abdullah Omar's rendering of *Jubang Linggang* is quite unlike that of Had, for, while the latter sings his story in the melody noted above, Abdullah Omar chants his version of the tale. The range of his chant is as follows:—

The range is within the interval of a minor sixth. The tonic is a perfect fourth from the lowest note, and the highest note is a perfect fourth from the tonic. There are only six notes involved, with the flattened leading-note and flattened third producing the tune's character. The tune lingers about the tonic, super-tonic and leading-note. Quite often, the flattened third (i.e. B♭) is used in the form of *apoggiatura* as decoration of the super-tonic. The pattern thus produced may be used in the middle of a passage or it may occur as a final cadence. The perfect fourth above the tonic is sometimes used as the opening after the final cadence. The resulting rhythm is irregular and the phrases are unevenly balanced.

Tales delivered in repetitive chant are also found in Pahang, Trengganu and Perlis. Esah (Pahang) performs both her stories *(Raja Donan* and *Siti Jalan)* in chant, and here, again, each story has its own specific melody. In *Raja Donan*, the range is as follows:

The tune is chanted within the range of an interval of a minor sixth, consisting of three notes. The tonic is at the middle of the range, a diminished fourth from the lowest note, and a major third from the top note. The tune lingers about the tonic and the top note, and they are prolonged and repeated as reciting notes.

The *Selampit* of Perlis also chants his stories. The tale of *Selindung Bulan Kedah Tua* is intoned in two alternating[25] phrases of melody. The reciting note in both is the super-tonic. In the one phrase, the opening is on the tonic, in which case the final cadence ends on the same note as the reciting note; in the other phrase, the opening is pitched above the reciting note, whereupon the cadence is on the tonic. Each phrase is usually broken into two or three parts, the last one being the shortest, but this does not disrupt the regularity of the rhythm. It may be noted that Ismail employs the same chant for both his stories, that mentioned above and *Si Suton*. However, as in the case of singing, two performers presenting the same tale may

---

[25] However, the same phrase sometimes appears consecutively.

employ a different melody. Thus, Bahtin of Langkawi, when performing the same tale as *Selindung Bulan Kedah Tua* (although under a different name: *Terung Pipit*) does not use the same chant as Ismail. The other Perlis story-teller of the *Selampit* type, Isahak, also intones his tale in a chant. In his rendering of *Malim Deman*, the reciting note is the mediant. Each passage consists of a series of repeated short phrases or motifs of uneven length which usually open on the tonic, ascend to the reciting note and finally descend again to the tonic. He ends the passage with a cadence produced by prolonging the final reciting note and the tonic. In the excerpts (Pr. 2), commas are used to delimit the short phrases.

The intonation of the *Awang Batil* differs somewhat from the previous examples. Here, the rhythm of speech or chant is determined by the beat of the *batil* upon which the performer strums continuously. The tale is intoned in passages. Each passage commences with a prolonged opening note and ends with a cadence. In the case of Mahmud, however, apart from the opening and the cadence, the passage is delivered in rhythmic speech: each phrase carries two stresses and, in the majority of cases, contains two words. Mahmud uses this technique for all his tales. In the rendering of Fadhil, we again find the two-word clusters but these also are chanted. He, too, uses the same chant for other tales.

2. Variability of form

We shall now examine the question of how fixed is the form of the *penglipur lara* tale. In each of the examples presented below (Ph. 3 — Kd. 3), extracts from two performances of the same tale by the same story-teller are presented for comparison. We see that the form of the tales is by no means fixed, and there is no question of the story-teller learning the tale by heart in the manner of one who studies the *Qur'an* until he is word perfect. On the other hand, there is a good deal more similarity in wording between two renderings of the same *penglipur lara* tale than between two performances of the same *wayang kulit* drama by the same *dalang* (see Sweeney, 1972), where the language used is different each time and only the content of the drama remains relatively constant. There are, of course, passages fixed in form in both *wayang kulit* and *penglipur lara*, such as the descriptions in so-called 'rhythmical prose'. Here, however, we are concerned with the language in which the body of the narrative is delivered.

The impression one receives from listening to repeated performances of one tale by the same story-teller is that each rendering is a paraphrase of an imaginary 'master-copy', so that in the parallel parts of two performances almost every sentence of the one rendering has its counterpart in the other, and, although different in wording and often in sequence, both sentences will usually have a number of words in common; in some instances phrases, clauses and even whole sentences are almost identical in form. Although these remarks apply to the performances of all the story-tellers examined, comparison of renderings reveals that some performers display a higher degree of constancy than others. Thus, for example, the renderings of Had's *Raja Lotong* (Kd. 2) are less variable in form than those of Hasan bin Adam (Ph. 3).

A further qualification is that two renderings of a tale by the same performer do not usually exhibit the same rate of constancy throughout the performance. It is the beginning which possesses the greatest constancy of form. This is due to the facts that a) stories are often introduced with opening formulae, fairly fixed in form (see page 25), and b) the story-teller is particularly alert at the beginning of his performance, for this is the key to the tale and he must ensure that the stage is set correctly for the subsequent unfolding of the plot. Thus, in our extracts, we see that it is the opening lines which display the highest degree of uniformity.

Furthermore, although we have likened each rendering to a paraphrase of an imaginary 'master-copy', which represents the story-teller's total knowledge of the tale, conscious selection and vagaries of memory will ensure that a rendering differs somewhat from previous performances: details may vary, episodes may be omitted here, included there, and sections may be abridged or expanded. However, as such variability of form and content does not usually appear in the opening stages of a performance, and can only be satisfactorily appreciated from the comparison of two complete renderings of a tale, which forms the subject of part II of this paper, detailed comment on these features will be reserved until then. Nevertheless, certain of our examples reveal considerable variation quite early in the story. For example, the extract from the third rendering of Isahak's *Malim Deman* is only about one fifth of the length of the parallel part of the other two renderings (Pr. 2). And the two renderings of Abdullah Omar's *Jubang Linggang*, after a very similar opening, branch off into different episodes.

A final factor, though not, apparently, a major one, is the time interval between performances. In some cases two renderings performed within a day or so revealed more similarity than with a third rendering performed a year later. This is seen in Had's case: the two renderings of *Raja Lotong* were recorded on the one visit. There was a time interval of six years, however, between the two recordings of *Jubang Linggang*. There is more similarity between the first two than between the latter two renderings. A third rendering of Raja Lotong a year later revealed slightly more variation than between the first two, but a third recording of *Jubang Linggang* a year later showed only about the same degree of variation as between the previous two. In the case of the other story-tellers examined, two renderings performed within twenty-four hours revealed as much variation as those recorded a year later.

3. Co-ordination of words and music

As we have seen, the performer does not learn off lines by rote, so there is no question of his merely churning out lyrics previously dove-tailed to the melody. Each rendering is a re-creation of the story and the story-teller faces the task of co-ordinating words to melody on each occasion he performs. The fixed opening formula enables him to 'get into gear' smoothly. Then, having achieved the desired rhythm and tempo, he proceeds to employ what we may term 'co-ordinating devices'. These are of two types: one entails distortion of the melody, the other of the words, and the performer may employ either or both of these. An example of the former is Jidin's *Raja Gagak* (Ph. 1). We notice that there is considerable disparity in the length of lines sung to the same stretch of melody; compare for example the lines:

nak kemana ng aya ke.. du.. li and
lalu dibelahnya nga habis segala isi perut dikeluarkannya belaka.. semua.. nya..

This is made possible by repeating or prolonging certain notes. Consequently there is considerable irregularity of the rhythm. Furthermore, the fourth line, which is omitted on occasion, is delivered in a monotone and its function may be likened to an overflow tank, which accomodates whatever could not be squeezed into the preceding three lines.

On the other hand, the performer may preserve the rhythm of the melody at the expense of the words used. An example of this is Hasan's *Burung Agut* (Ph. 3). Here, the lines are much more uniform in length. This is achieved by inserting a variety of 'fillers' or 'balancing words', often meaningless, such as *la nya* and *wei*. The performer may use both devices at once. Thus Jidin's *Burung Agut* (Ph. 2) employs a certain amount of prolongation but is a good deal more regular in rhythm than his *Burung Gagak*. He also uses a number of 'fillers' such as *la nya*, *nga 'ni* and *amboi*. Even in *Burung Gagak* fillers are not entirely absent.

Another way of co-ordinating words and music, which also entails distortion of the language, is to abandon all attempt to ensure that the end of a stretch of the melody coincides with a natural pause of the utterance. The performer is thus largely able to dispense with fillers and yet maintain a regular rhythm. The stretches of utterance, however, are prone to be cut off abruptly and continued in the following phrase of the melody. In extreme examples, as that of Had (Kd. 2 & 3), words may even be split in half.

In stories which are chanted, the performer, when seeking a convenient place to end a passage with a cadence, merely prolongs the duration of the reciting note. In the *Awang Batil*, with its short phrases consisting mainly of two equally stressed words, the performer is able to continue indefinitely until he decides on a final cadence. Fillers are also employed in chanted stories. For example, Ismail uses *no*, *kal* etc.; Isahak uses *lo;* Abdullah Omar: *wei;* Esah: *la*. Mahmud, too, employs them, to balance the two halves of his phrases, for example: *a oh*, *che'*, etc.

4. Language

Before discussing the language of the *penglipur lara*, I would refer the reader to my remarks on the language of the Malay shadow-play, the *wayang Siam* (Sweeney, 1972: 63–72), as several features are common to both. The story-teller presents the tale in his own dialect for, as in the case of the *dalang*, he and his audience are usually unfamiliar with classical or literary Malay. In the *wayang*, we find that *dalangs* produce a heightened form of local dialect by introducing various distortions of grammar, both through ignorance and design. This feature is also sometimes found in the language of the story-teller, but on a much more modest scale. Nevertheless, the exigencies of the relatively formal context ensure that his language is more high-flown than usual. He will often use affixes and particles not found in his everyday speech and this may result in some singular forms. Thus, for example, we encounter usages such as *meadil ke nya* (= *mengadilkannya*) (Ph. 1.17), *digelaran* (Pr. 1.A.41), *berdengan* (Pr. 2.B.80), *mengayah* (= *ayah*) (Ph. 2.35), *tu-dari, bertujuh* (Kd. 2.A.3;50), *tu-dengan* (Kd. 1.A.1). The pronunciation of words may be distorted, e.g. *baatera* (= *berita*) (Kd. 1.A.1), *betera* (= *putera*) (Pr. 1.A.40); and story-tellers, when singing or chanting, commonly prefix the phoneme ŋ to words beginning with a vowel. This feature, which is designed to increase the sonority of the word, is also found in *wayang* singing (e.g. see Sweeney, 1972: 349).

Contortions of syntax also result in constructions which would not be found in everyday speech. For example, *Dan pada malam inilah tuan oi kami, dan nak dengar cherita...* (Pr. 1.B.7). Ismail often 'misuses' *dan* in this fashion. Also: *Berapa diseronok berapa diramai apa disait dikait,* (Pr. 2.B.20).

In common also with the *dalang* of the *wayang*, the story-teller sometimes employs special words not found in everyday speech, which the story-teller himself cannot always explain or to which he may ascribe an idiosyncratic meaning. Examples of such words are *deksa* (Kd.2.A.10), *gindang, botera* (Pr.1.A.16;5) and, in Perlis and Pahang, where it is not part of the dialect, the Kelantanese-Patani *royat* (Pr. 3) & (Ph. 3).

In respect of both distortion and special words, the language of the *tarik Selampit* is closer to the *wayang Siam* than are the other genres of story-telling, and will be examined in part II of this paper.

The story-teller usually unfolds the content of his story quite slowly. This need not mean that his rate of delivery is slow, for he may be reciting at quite a rapid pace; rather he tends to spread the content thinly by employing repetition and a variety of padding devices. This is necessary for two reasons. Firstly, audience conditions are far more informal than say in a modern concert-hall where the audience is lined up in rows and hardly dares to cough; at a traditional story-telling session, one may expect a whole range of background noises, from babies screaming to toothless old men pounding their *sirih*. Consequently, one does not expect to catch the story-teller's every word. Secondly, the performer is faced with the dual tasks of marshalling the threads of his tale and then co-ordinating them with his song or chant. As it is essential for a professional story-teller to maintain his flow of language and never hesitate, he avails himself of some 'elbow room' by the use of repetition and padding.

We have noticed the use of 'fillers' to co-ordinate words with music. The story-teller also employs meaningless phrases composed of such words in order to allow himself a moment's breathing space to think of a name or of what to say next and, indeed, some fillers perform a dual function. Examples of such phrases are *Che' Na, sedang tatkala* (Pr. 2.B.33;1); *sedang a kal, sedang a nya, tuan oi* (Pr. 1. *passim*). Sometimes the performer does not use such a phrase but invents a nonsense utterance as the need arises; for example: *amboi juga nga la nga nya nga ke ng ini* (Ph. 2. 27), *aya juga ng amboi 'ni* (Ph. 1. 3).[26]

---

[26] In some melodies he is also free to 'hang on to' a syllable by lengthening the note on which it is sung.

Performers usually employ a good deal of repetition. This may entail recounting the same details in different words as, for example, in Jidin's *Burung Gagak* (Ph. 1.5–16) or merely repeating an utterance verbatim; for example, *Patik bertangguhlah malam esok* (Ph. 4.A. 84). There are, however, a variety of rather more stylized techniques. The performer may employ a string of synonyms where one word would suffice as, for example, *chetera hikayat bari* (Kd. 1.A.7), *sejurus sejenang* (Ph. 4.A.44), *anak dengan putera* (Pr. 2.A.10).

Synonyms are not always just strung together. Sometimes, part of an utterance is repeated verbatim while a synonym is substituted for the remaining part. For example, *nanti hari nanti ketika* (Kd. 1.B.32); *satu royat satu chetera* (Kd. 1.A.9). When each of the parts of such constructions corresponds to a phrase or half-phrase of the melody, the utterances produce parallelisms. The repetition usually occurs at the beginning, resulting in anaphora, e.g. *pada 'tika 'ni, pada waktu 'ni* (Pr. 3.A.12); *ada satu konon, ada satu chetera* (Pr. 2.1); *la panjang royat, la panjang la cherita/ panjang royat panjang la chetera* (Ph. 3.A.5).

The performer may also use parallelisms as a way of developing the plot in a leisurely manner. Here, the variable part of the construction will not contain a synonym, but a word or phrase which carries the story forward. Examples are:— *Tabik segala ng orang wei sekalian./Tabik segala ng orang di kayangan.* (anaphora. Ph. 3.B.2); *masuk hutan, keluar hutan* (epiphora. Fadhil, Langkawi); *habis padang, masuk kampung, habis kampung, habis padang,....* (anaphora and epiphora. Pr. 3.B.91); *chari pagi, duk makan, che' pagi, chari dah petang, duk makan, che' petang.* (anaphora & *reponsie*,[27] Pr. 3.B.62.); *hang tengok aku, aku tengok hang* (responsie. Pr. 3.A. 17); *mana tak kena, pakat tolong, pekena,/mana tak betul, pakat tolong, perbetul* (anaphora and *responsie*. Pr. 3.A. 25); *nak timbul, timbul pula, (woordopname.* Pr. 3.B. 51); *Raja nama....../negeri bernama....../ permaisuri nama.......* (*responsie*. Pr. 2. B.3); *Ng amboi ng adik apalah..../ Ng amboi kanda jikalau...* (anaphora, Ph. 4.B. 7); *Ada bulan Rabi-awal/ dua-belas bulan Rabi-awal* (epiphora, Ph. 4.A. 6); *Biar ng hilang la nya jiwa..../ biar padi padang jarak.../ biar ng hitam asap lotong...* (anaphora, Ph. 2.40); *putera dia ng ada la nya seorang/Putera dia saja wei la nya seorang* (symploke, Ph. 3.A. 22). Sometimes a performer has a stock parallelism, as in the case of Hasan (Ph. 3. 20): *semangkin.... semangkin...,* which is used on many occasions.

We find that such parallelisms occur where the rhythm of the song or chant is regular, resulting in evenly balanced stretches of utterance. In the great majority of cases, each part of the parallelism is a meaningful entity. A curious exception is found in the performance of Had (Kd. 2 & 3). As a result of his method of delivery, discussed above, we encounter forms such as: *ei hamba ambil pula, si jala/ ei besar jala besar, si jala* (symploke); *lama dua kali bertujuh/ hari dua kali bertujuh* (epiphora); *ei Besar chapai pula, ke jala/ ei besar duduk champak, dilubuk/ ei besar lubuk besar, si batu/ ei besar sangat lama, sejulung* (anaphora). We also find parallelisms used extensively in fixed passages, which will now be discussed.

---

[27] As I am not aware of English equivalents, I have employed the Dutch terms (see e.g. Bijleveld, 1943).

Passages which are fixed in form consist of, on the one hand, various types of stock phrase and 'rhythmical prose', which have an independent existence in so far as they may be used whenever necessary in a story, and, on the other, opening formulae, which only occur at the beginning[28] and which, apart from the first three or four lines, are prone to variation, in some cases being only relatively more fixed in form than the subsequent parts of the story.

Two types of opening formula are commonly found: the *konon* and the *tabik* types. The *konon* formula is very simple and merely consists of one or two short phrases containing the word *konon* ('It is said'). The performer may employ the same formula for several stories, although it is subject to minor variation to ensure that the words accord with the dictates of the rhythm of a particular story, and slight variation may even occur between two renderings of the same tale. Thus, for example, Esah (Ph. 4.) uses: *Ada konon la tidak konon, ada masa suatu masa* for *Raja Donan*, which is lengthened by the use of fillers when used in *Siti Jalan: Amboi lah ng ada konon tidak konon, ng ada masa suatu masa*. And in four samples of *Raja Donan*, two were as the above, but on the third occasion the form was: *Ada konon suatu konon, ada masa la tidak masa,* and on the fourth: *Ada konon la tidak konon, ada masa suatu malam.*

Similarly, Jidin's basic formula is *Ada konon tak konon....* (*Bongsu Pinang Peribut*), but this, again, may vary between renderings and in different tales. Where the rhythm produces a longer phrase we may get *Adalah konon sitidaklah konon* (*Raja Muda*). And in *Burung Agut*, the formula differs further: *Aya nga pun konon....* In general, *konon* formulae are found in the more modest presentations. Thus, Isahak (Pr. 2.) also uses a *konon* formula: *Ada suatu konon ada suatu cherita.*

Tabik are usually a good deal longer than *konon* formulae, and often only the first few lines are really fixed. Even in the simplest form encountered, that of Hasan (Ph. 3.), two renderings showed considerable variation after the first two lines. The longer *tabik* of Ismail and Mahmud also reveal considerable variation. In that of Abdullah Omar (Kd. 1.), although the words are almost identical in each rendering, the co-ordination of words to chant varies noticeably. The *tabik* of Had (Kd. 2.) is longer but also varies little, partly due to the fact that it contains a *pantun*. The story-tellers interviewed use the same *tabik* for more than one tale, with only the same variation as found in two renderings of the same tale.

After the *konon* or *tabik* formula, the story itself commences. Here we sometimes find that the opening lines are fixed, and may be regarded as a part of the opening formula, as with Isahak (see his three renderings, Pr. 2.), and Abdullah Omar (Kd. 1.). In most instances, however, this is not so, and the greater constancy of form in the opening over subsequent parts of the tale is, as noted above, only a matter of degree.

We have already mentioned the use of nonsense phrases to afford the performer a moment's respite. Often similar in function, but differing in that they are meaningful in their contexts and may have aesthetic appeal, are a number of stock phrases and clichés, some of which are also found in the same form in the *wayang Siam*. Examples of such stock phrases are: *timur barat selatan dengan utara* (Pr. 1.B. 50),

---

[28] However, some performers employ the same formula in more than one story.

bukan alang kepalang (Ph. 1. 16), *bidan ketujuh bidan ketiga; nujum nerus nujum ketika; karam tak berayar bakar tak berapi gantung tak bertali* (Pr. 2.A. 25;36;51), *riuh dan rendah gegak gemita* (Pr. 3.A. 14), *berjalan belang melenggang* (Kd. 2.A. 46); *dua kali bertujuh hari dua kali bertujuh malam* (Kd. 3.B. 70); *sial di mana majal di mana* (Kd. 3.B. 36); *apa bala dengan chentaka* (Kd. 3.A. 38). We note in excerpts (Kd. 2 & 3) that constructions which are parallelisms in normal speech will often not appear as such when sung by Had, as a result of his method of splitting his utterances.

Some words are regularly followed by a short description, as *bahtera kurang sa seratus genap* (Ph. 4.A. 88); similarly, very long names are sometimes found, which is also a feature of the *wayang Siam*. An extreme case of this is in Abdullah Omar (Kd. 1.A.11;26), where the names of the land Tanjung Luluk and the *jong* (boat) become long descriptions in 'rhythmical prose'. Furthermore, lists of objects may form stock phrases, e.g. *dian tanglung pelita* (Ph. 4.A. 45), and the strings of synonyms, mentioned above, often fossilize into such phrases.

Two types of stock phrase possessing special functions are what may be termed scene-openers and closers, and frame-phrases. Examples of the former are: *hilang al-kesah......, nak timbul pula sedang a cherita* (Pr. 1.A.23); *hilang royat, berita, nak timbul, timbul tersebut.....*(Pr. 3.A. 58); *nak timbul satu royat* (Kd. 1.B. 8); *hilang royat hilang cherita timbul tersebut* (Kd. 3.B. 2); *hilang royat timbul cherita* (Ph. 3.A. 8). They are employed to indicate the end of one section of the narrative and the commencement of another, and may be compared to chapter headings and rubrication in written literature. They are also used in the *wayang Siam*, where the commonest scene-closer and opener are respectively *hilang royat* and *timbul cherita*. It should be noted that the word *royat* is not normally used in the dialects of Mahmud or Hasan and its use in these phrases reveals Kelantan-Patani influence.

The second type is the frame phrase. We have seen that, musically speaking, our stories are strophic, i.e. one passage of music is repeated over and over again. In some cases, the beginning and end of this passage are signalled not only on the musical level by a special pattern of notes, but also on the level of utterance, by the use of special phrases. These are also repeated throughout the story and form thus a 'framework' for the narrative. Examples are: *Oh oh o..h nik o..h* [...] *wei* [...] at the beginning and *wei... / Timang* [...] *nik der, / ayo dendang, / che' dondang di, / di dondang* at the end of each passage (Kd. 2), and *Oh oh o..h nik o..h* (beginning), *'ni ga'* [...] (end) (Kd. 3).

In *Awang Batil*, too, we see that each passage is introduced with *hei..* (Mahmud, Pr. 3.) or *hei.. ei.. ei.. ei...* (Fadhil, Langkawi).

Similar in function to frame-phrases is the use of rhyme in 'a' by Ismail and Isahak of Perlis. Ismail concludes every passage with a rhyming word. At first sight, this seems a very formidable task, in view of the fact that the performer has not learn his tale by rote. Actually, however, Ismail has little difficulty, for he has at his finger-tips a large number of words rhyming in 'a', including several 'stand-by' words which can be used in any contingency, such as *semula, yang manakan ada, apatah kira* etc. Indeed, he derives enormous amusement from talking to guests in similar rhymed phrases. Isahak also employs rhyme in 'a', but is not so consistent in its use as Ismail. Only about half of his short phrases end in 'a'. The final cadence terminating each passage often ends in such a rhyme, but on numerous occasions a proper name (not rhyming in 'a') concludes the passage.

Last, but by no means least, we shall discuss what is commonly known as 'rhythmical prose'. This term is generally used to refer to the descriptive passages in set form which occur regularly in the various 'folk-romances' edited by British Colonial scholars, and which are printed in the form of blank verse. Thus, Hooykaas, basing his conclusions on the form of such passages in the published tales, states:
"Een eigenaardigheid in stijl, waardoor zich deze verhalen onderscheiden van alle andere Maleise literatuur is deze, dat traditionele beschrijvingen worden opgenomen in korte regeltjes, waarvan de woorden ontegenzegglijk enigszins assoneren, maar niet rijmen."[29] (Hooykaas, 1947: 49–50).
And Winstedt calls them 'metrical passages inset in these romances by their Sumatran reciters[30] (Winstedt, 1958: 31). By 'inset', he means that the bulk of the story is told in prose and that 'only the metrical parts are handed down exactly in set traditional forms' (Winstedt 1957a: 149). This, then, is the generally accepted view of what is meant by 'rhythmical prose.' It is apparently the belief that a *penglipur lara* tale should contain such passages of brief non-rhyming phrases which has led subsequent editors to print arbitrarily in short lines anything that vaguely resembles 'rhythmical prose', regardless of whether this is justified by the original recital or whether the language is fixed in form. Thus, in certain tales, such as *Raja Gagak* (Zaharah Taha, 1963), passages of dialogue are confused with rhythmical prose, and in others, e.g. *Raja Dera* (Nik Maimunah, 1962), all dialogue is printed in short lines.

Winstedt's idea that these passages are metrical islands in a sea of prose is based on his examination of the non-stylized form alone. As we have seen (page 4), an 'off-duty' professional, or an amateur familiar with the stories may well recount them in everyday speech but including such passages at relevant points. In the stylized form, however, i.e. in a professional performance, the whole tale is intoned in a specific melody, and there is absolutely no difference in rhythm or intonation between these passages of 'rhythmical prose' and the rest of the tale. The use of the terms 'rhythmical prose' or 'metrical parts' to distinguish these descriptive passages in fixed form is therefore misleading, for the whole story is presented in the same 'rhythmical prose'.

Furthermore, the idea that these fixed descriptive passages are spoken in short lines requires some qualification. In discussing the question of the delimitation of stretches of utterance in the tale as a whole, we saw that the length of an utterance is determined by the duration of the phrase of melody, although usually with an

---

[29] "A peculiarity of style, distinguishing these tales from all other Malay literature is this, that traditional descriptions are presented in short lines, the words of which, to a certain extent, unquestionably assonate, but do not rhyme."

[30] With regard to Sumatran origin of stories, it may be noted that in Pahang, several tales (but by no means all) are said to be Minangkabau in origin, e.g. *Bongsu Pinang Peribut* and *Raja Muda* (according to Jidin). And Esah's grandfather, from whom she obtained *Raja Donan*, was a Minangkabau. We note in the latter case the short lines used are very reminiscent of the Minangkabau *kaba*. (Cf. Hooykaas (1961:90), who suggested such a possibility,)

allowance for variation within a certain range.[31] This is also the case with fixed passages. In those tales where the phrases of melody are quite short, as in examples collected in Pahang, the fixed descriptive passages are presented in short, fairly evenly-balanced stretches of the *yang buta datang bertongkat* type, of which a considerable number contain four (and sometimes three) words. The flexibility of length, within certain limits, of the stretches of utterance in these tales enables the performer to employ the same fixed passages in more than one tale, so that some of these descriptions, e.g. the *yang buta datang bertongkat* variety, have very wide circulation. And, although the same passages may be intoned to various rhythms, including that of normal speech in an informal context, we often find that their form as parallelisms is emphasized and preserved by the use of devices such as anaphora, epiphora etc. Where these devices are not used, variation may occur, even when recited in the one tale as, for example, in the case of Esah (Ph. 4.A&B) where we find on one occasion: *lagi jauh berserang dekat / sudah dekat berserang sampai* and on another: *lagi jauh berdatang sembah / sudah dekat tersunjang lutut 'ngan dua* (the *ter-* is not strong enough to preserve a parallel with *terangkat*). And even when such devices are used, the phrases are still prone to internal variation for, although 'fixed', their form is by no means inviolate, and their sequence in passages often varies; compare, for example, Esah's two renderings (Ph. 4.A & B).[32] Nevertheless, the length is still fairly uniform.

In a number of tales, the phrases of the melody produce stretches of utterance which are well outside the range of the *yang buta datang bertongkat* type. When this type is to be used in such a tale, therefore, some modification is necessary. This may be illustrated by the three examples from Perlis. In each of the three tales there is the description: *Ayam berkokok murai membacha / fajar menyingsing atas kepala.* This is within the range of Isahak's phrases and appears in exactly this form (Pr. 2.A. 71).[33] When it is used by Ismail, who produces much longer phrases, however, it is lengthened by the use of 'fillers' and the inclusion of extra details, thus: *Dan besok hari, hari pun dah siang, ayam pun berkokok, murai pun semua 'ni sedang a membacha / Dan fajar menyingsing tuan oi merah, sedang a bernyala.* (Pr. 1.A. 54) When the utterance produced is shorter, as in the case of Mahmud, the phrase is bisected, thus: *ayam pun kokok / jarang jarang basa / murai 'mbacha / di luar pagar / fajar menyingsing / merah nyala.* (Pr.3.A.10).

When, however, the melody produces long, unevenly[34] balanced stretches of utterance, the form of the fixed passages is considerably different. Thus, for example, not only are Abdullah Omar's fixed passages not divided into balanced phrases; the delimitation of these phrases is not even constant, for the pauses dividing them are not bound to occur in the same places on each occasion, as comparison of the

---

[31] E.g. see *Burung Raja Gagak*, where lines are not uniform in length.
[32] And comparison of the various fixed passages in the *penglipur lara* tales of the *Malay Literature Series* reveals considerable variation.
[33] Isahak's phrases are not of uniform length, however, and it does not always appear in this form (see e.g. 2.B.63).
[34] Although Ismail's phrases are long, they are regular in rhythm and well-balanced. This regularity is reflected in the utterance by the use of rhyme and balancing words.

description of Tanjung Luluk reveals (Kd. 1.A. & B.). In this respect, Abdullah Omar's fixed passages resemble those of the *tarik Selampit*. Indeed the passage *Dia pun bersaksilah......hitam* (Kd. 1.B. 50) is almost identical with one used by Mat Nor (Kelantan). In the *tarik Selampit*, the performer does not employ a strophic technique, and the length of his utterances is not bound by the dictates of the melody; furthermore, his fixed passages are regularly spoken, and resemble thus the *bilangan* of the shadow-play (see Sweeney, 1972: 65–72). In both *tarik Selampit* and *wayang* the performer employs a strong, sometimes syncopated, rhythm, often gabbling the passage at great speed in the manner of the 'runs' of Gaelic tales. He is thus at complete liberty to vary the length of his utterances. He may, indeed, employ short, parallel phrases, as examination of the *bilangan* referred to above reveals, but he is not constrained to do so, and it is usual to find long and short stretches of utterance interspersed.

EXCERPTS

I have not employed phonetic transcription in the following excerpts, for, although a number of dialects are involved, my aim is not to undertake a linguistic analysis but to provide texts which are easily understood by the speaker of standard Malay. Nevertheless, attention is drawn in the notes to major deviations from standard Malay. At the beginning of each excerpt, the following information is given: the name of the performer, his established place of residence, approximate age, the title of the tale and the date of recording. A hyphen at the end of a word (or part of a word except at the end of a line) indicates a slip of the tongue. Coughing is indicated by the sign (c). Commas are only used to indicate actual pauses. Dots '..' after a vowel indicate that the syllable is prolonged. It may be noted here that after transcribing the recordings, I revisited the various performers in order to clear up obscurities of language etc.

Ph.1. Jidin bin Ali, Kuala Kaung, Temerloh, Pahang + 70
(ob. 1973)

BURUNG RAJA GAGAK
(March, 1972)

Adalah ko- konon tak kononnya.. te.. Gagak Pu- Raja.. Ga..gak
Gagak Putih dengan Gaga.k Hi..tam
Aya juga.. ng ambo..i 'ni..
la dia kata dia,

5 "Aya ingkang duli.. tua..nku
nak kemana ng aya ke.. du.li
apa susa.h la ng apa.. ga..duh
raja yang besar menakluk ne..ge..ri?"

"Amboi, susahnya ng aku bukan ala..ng kepa..lang
10 masa ini Raja Gagak Putih Gagak ng Hita.m
susahnya buka..nlah sebara..ng ba..rang."

Lalu dikatanya dek Gagak Putih Gaga..k ng Hi..tam
"Apa susah duli patik boleh di..ba..ntu
Cheritakanlah kepada pati..k sengkat mana.. yang a..da."

15 Lalu cherita dek Raja.. Be..sar
"Susah ng aku semasa sekarang ini bukan ng alang kepalang
memerentah ke negeri.. nak meadi..l ke.. nya."
Lalu kata dek Gagak Putih "Saya ke bawah duli,

Kalau sudah semacham itu tidak juga susah juga kepada.. pa..tik
20 chobalah patik kalau dibenarkan patik belah ba- perut duli.. tua..ku."
Seraya kata Raja Besar "Silalah belah peru..t ng a..ku
kerana ng aku susah fikiran sesak."

Lalu dibelah dek Raja.. dek Gagak Putih 'ngan Gaga..k ng Hi..tam
lalu dibelahnya nga habis segala isi perut dikeluarkannya belaka.. semua..nya..
25 Sudah dibasuh dilimau langir dichuchi..ka..n
Gagak Putih 'ngan Gagak Hitam lalu lah juga

segala menteri hulubalang, dia nak balik te- ke seberang laut terbang ambil
    obata..n yang ba..ik.
Lalu terbanglah dia Gagak Putih 'ngan Gagak Hitam sejurus sejenang panjang.

30 Balik ke seberang laut la nya.. ng i..tu
serta lalulah dia kembali pulang nga nya ke.mba.li
bawa dua kuntum bunga yang amat harum yang ama..t mele..mpah
lalu dimasuknya ke dalam perut raja ng itu.

Sudah dimasuknya lalu disapunya tiga kali dengan sehuju..ng sa..yap
35 baliklah dia aman sentosa seperti sedia.. 'ni ka..la
amboilah bukan lagi ng alang kepalanglah gaya segala rakyat menteri
    hulubalang suka..ri..anya
ke raja dia sedang elok kembali.

Ph.2. Jidin bin Ali

BURUNG AGUT
(March, 1972)

Aya nga pun kono..n
la nya Tuan la Puteri yang Bongsu..
ng anak kepada raja Raja la 'ni Besar
aya ng akan juga amboi la nya ng ini..
5 la juga la ng ada la nya juga
ala tengahlah bersiap la berlengka..p
nak berkahwin dengan amboi Raja Muda...

Raja Besar tidak mahu ke Burung Agu..t
"Ngapa pula la menantu ke burung barang
10 kalau muntah darah nga pun ulat semu..t
tempat tidur la nya tempat la 'ni berak
kutu banyak la nya hama la 'ni banya..k
ala juga macham mana nga nak mari makan **anak bini**...

Lagi nga pun malu la nya di aku..
15 nga menantu nga kan burung la 'ni bara..ng
macham tidak ng ada raja-raja yang nga besa..r
la nya juga la di dalam negeri ini
seluruh la nya juga la dunia..
ala bukan sikit ng orang raja-raja
20 ng awak pula la menantu burung bara..ng
hina sungguh la aib sungguh la nya juga..."

```
       Nak meraya ng akan juga ng ini..
       nga dengan hari la nya satu.. la ni ng hari..
       la nya datang la nya ng amboi putera nga nya
    25 ala bawa bekas sirih la sebiji..
       ala datang a mendapat ke ayahanda
       amboi juga nga la nga nya nga ke ng ini..
       lalu sujudlah di kaki ayahanda dia...

       "Ng amboi juga..
    30 minta ampun minta maaf la nya ng aya..h
       lagi ng hujung kaki sampai ng hujung rambut
       ala juga ng anakanda la ni ng aya..h
       putera tidak ng ada dua la ni tiga
       hanyalah ada seorang diri patik juga..
    35 ng ayah nga kan juga nga meng aya..h.

       Aya tidak mahu kahwin dengan nga abang Raja Muda..
       nak kahwin dengan abang Burung Agut
       biar ng hilang la nya jiwa la di dada..
       biar padi padang jarak padang tekuku..r.

    40 Biar ng hitam asap lotong la nya ng ini..
       nga di dalam la negeri nga nya ng ini..
       kelam kabut la nya juga nga meng ayah
       ala biarlah menjadi padang jarak padang tekuku..r
       la baru puas ng hati la ni ng ayah
    45 ayah melaga segala rakyat-ayat ten-tentera..
       orang melaga la kerbau la ni kambing
       ng ayah nga melaga rakyat-ayat tentera hulubala..ng
       sebab anak kahwin dengan abang Burung Agut
       biar ng hilang sampai ng hilang jiwa di dada..
    50 tidak mahu la nya kahwin dengan orang lai..n."
```

Ph.3. **Hassan bin Adam**, Kertau, Temerloh, Pahang. ± 50

SI BURUNG AGUT

A (4th March 1972)	B (4th March 1972)
Tabik ng enche-e', tabik la nya tuan. Tabik segala ng orang wei la sekalia..n, kechil besar, tua la dan muda.	Tabik ng enche-e', tabik la nya tuan. Tabik segala ng orang wei la sekalia..n. Tabik segala ng orang di kayangan.
Tabik segala hamba wei la dan sahaya. 5 La panjang royat, la panjang la cherita.., Panjang roya-a-at panjang la chetera.	La kechil besar la tua la dan muda, jantan betina belaka la wei semua... Hilang royat timbul la cherita.
Halang iya- Hilang royat la timbul la cherita. Adalah kesah suatu la nya raja.., 10 Raja ng Agut tengah la wei awang-awang.	La hilang royat la timbul la chetera. Terbit la kesah suatu la negeri.., ah negeri di kayangan.

Anak raja la si Burung la nya ng Agut.
Anak raja muda ng atas la kayanga..n;
nama dia la Si Burung la nya ng Agut.

Mak inang dia Si Burung la nya Bayan.
15 ala tiga dengan la Si Burung la nya Mura..i.
Raja muda la Si Burung la nya ng Agut.

Hilang la kesah, timbul wei la cherita.
La Raja Besar ng atas wei la kayanga..n,
Semangkin lama, semangkin la nya tua.
20 Semangkin lama, semangkin tak terdaya.
Tak ada la siapa nak diharap la kan dia..,
putera dia ng ada la nya seorang.

Putera dia saja wei la nya seorang.
Ah betina tidak, jantan pun la nya tida..k.
25 Itu saja yang ada la nya dia.

Semangkin lama Raja wei la nya Besar,
lalu la dia beroyat berchetera..
kepada ng anak la Si Burung la nya ng Agut.

"Ng anak ng anak kepada la nya kami.
30 Ah dengar dengar ng aku la wei la berita..,
ng aku sekarang semangkin la nya tua."

Namalah Raja Besar di dalam la negeri,
semangkin lama, semangkin la nya tua..;
lama dapat seorang la putera.

Lalu digelar la Si Burung la nya ng Agut.
Gelaran nama Si Burung la nya ng Agu..t.
Mak inang dia la Si Burung la nya Bayan.

Mak inang dia la Si Burung la nya Murai;
semangkin lama, semangkin la nya besa..r.
Semangkin lama, semangkin la nya molek.

Ah bijak sungguh la Raja Si Burung ng Agut,
la bulu dia bulu wei la nya ng ema..s,
la mata dia mata la nya ng intan.

Semangkin lama, semangkin la gembera.
Semangkin lama, semangkin la nya suka...
Ayahanda dia wei nya la tu lagi.

Lama la ng ayah raja wei la nya dia,
lalu berkhabar kepada ng anak dia..,
"Ng anak ng anak kepada la nya ng aku.

Aku sekarang b- terlampau la nya susah;
aku sekarang terlampau la nya tua...,
siapa nga la nak ganti la nya ng aku?"

Ph. 4. **Esah binti Mat Akil,** Chenor, Temerloh, Pahang. + 60

RAJA DONAN

A	B
(March, 1972)	(March, 1973)

Ada konon la tidak konon,
ada masa suatu masa,
tengah malam la sunyi senyap
Ng ber-
5 Bermimpilah Datuk Raja Diu.
Ada bulan Rabi-awal
dua-belas bulan Rabi-awal
tengah malam la dini ng hari.
"Ng amboi ya ng adik Puteri la Gedung Batu
10 bangunlah ng adik la abang me ng apa takbir mimpi ng abang.
Bulan empat-belas jatuh ke riba,
chindai jantan melilit pinggang,
keris chabut di dalam sarung.
15 Ng apa nga la adik takbir mimpi kanda."

Ada konon la tidak konon,
ada masa suatu masa,
bermimpilah Raja Diu
bulan empat-belas jatuh ke riba,
chindai jantan melilit pinggang,
keris terchabut di dalam sarung.
"Ng amboi ng adik apalah adik ma- takbir mimpi kanda?"
"Ng amboi kanda jikalau begitu pesan la ayah 'ngan bonda,
kita nak dapat ng anak laki-laki."
"Baiklah ng adik...
Bangun nga lah ng adik pasang dian tanglung pelita."
Digerakkan mak inang,

Tengah malam la dini ng hari,
ada konon suatu konon,
ada masa la tidak masa,
bangkit nga la Siti Gedung Batu.
20 "Ng apa nga la ng adik termimpi m- takbir mimpi kanda.
Ng amboi ya kanda jaman ng ayah la dengan bonda,
takbir mimpi kanda petua nak dapat ng anak lelaki
25 sehabis bertuah sehabis molek."
"Baiklah ng adik .."
Anak perempuan adalah tujuh ng orang.
Raja Diu nak hendak ke n anak lelaki,
30 puas sudah bertapa dia
tidak dapat n anak laki-laki.
Takbir mimpi- (c)
"Takbir mimpi kanda kita nak dapat ng anak lelaki."
35 "Ng amboi ng adik." Jikalau begitu dia pergi nga la ke bilik ng air
teriak "Mak inang, pasanglah mak inang dian tanglung pelita."
"Apalah kehendak Duli Tuanku?"
40 "Hendak berpasal takbir mimpi kanda.
Dia mimpi bulan empat-belas jatuh ke riba,
keris terchabut di dalam sarung,
chindai jantan melilit pinggang."
Sejurus sejenang panjang bangunlah mak inang masang dian tanglung pelita.
45
Bangkit nga lah Raja Besar dua suami isteri,
pergi bersiram ke bilik mandi.
"Ng amboi kanda baik benar takbir kanda.
Ng amboi kanda." "Kalau begitu ng adik,
50 kita pukul chanang pemanggil."
Disahut
tabuh di ladang, dengan buta datang berpimpin,
dengan pekak terteleng-teleng,
55 dengan kurap memiah jalan,
dengan patah datang bertongkat,
lagi jauh berserang dekat,
sudah dekat berserang sampai,
tersunjang lutut 'ngan dua,
60 terangkat kadam sepuluh,
"Sembah Duli tuanku, harap nga kan di ng ampun.
Ng apa nga lah dipanggil patik?

dipasang dian tanglung pelita,
Bangkit nga lah Raja Diu pergi ke kolam bersiram d- dua suami isteri.
Sudah bersiram, "Ng amboi ng adik." "Apalah kanda?"
"Baiklah pukul chanang pemanggil."
Disahut tabuh di ladang,
dengan buta datang berpimpin,
dengan pekak terteleng-teleng,
dengan patah datang bertongkat,
dengan kurap memiah jalan,
lagi jauh berdatang sembah,
sudah dekat tersunjang lutut 'ngan dua,
terangkat kadam sepuluh.
"Sembah ng ampun beribu ng ampun,
harap di ng ampun duli tuanku,
ng apa dipanggil la patik ini?
Di mana kota la dengan roboh?
Di mana parit la dengan semak?
Di mana dinding dengan rabang?
Di mana lantai 'ngan jungkang jungkit?
Di mana di- ng atap 'ngan bintang-bintang?"
"Taada ng atap 'ngan bintang-bintang,
taada lantai 'ngan jungkang jungkit,
taada dinding dengan rabang,
taada kota la dengan sebu,
taada parit la dengan roboh.
Kami memanggil ng awak semua
'ngajak pergi memikat ke Gunung Sangga Lotang,
mimpi denak banyak sangat di situ."
"Duli tuanku sembah patik beribu ng ampun
sembah patik ng harap di ng ampun,
patik bertangguh nga la malam esok."
"Tidak ngapa nga lah awak semua,
siapkan deras bahtera kita,
bahtera kurang sa seratus genap.
Kami hendak pergi memikat ke Gunung Sangga Lotang,
denak banyak sangat di situ."
"Tidak ngapa nga lah duli tuanku."
Sejurus sejenang panjang,
berkerahlah hulubalang perdana menteri,
menyiapkan bahtera kurang sa seratus genap.

Di mana kota la dengan sebu?
65 Di mana parit la dengan roboh?
Di mana ng atap 'ngan bintang-bintang?
Di mana dinding dengan rabang?
Di mana ng atap dengan bintang-bintang?
Di mana lantai dengan jungkang jungkit?"
70 "Ng amboi ke taada lantai dengan jungkang jungkit,
taada dinding dengan rabang,
taada parit la dengan sebu,
taada kota dengan roboh,
75 taada- Kami memanggil ng awak semua 'ngajak
pergi kami ke Gunung Ledang
kami ke Gunung Sangga Lotang,
kami hendak pergi memikat ke situ mimpi
80 kami denak banyak
sangat di Gunung Sangga Lotang."
"Duli tuanku sembah ampun beribu ng ampun,
patik bertangguhlah malam esok.
85 Patik bertangguhlah malam esok."
Sampai malam esok datang nga la ng orang membela Bédar Palembang
bela bahtera kurang sa seratus
genap Raja Diu nak berangkat ke Gunung
90 Sangga Lotang.

Pr. I. **Ismail bin Hassan**, Kurong Batang, Perlis, ± 70

SELINDUNG BULAN KEDAH TUA

A
(March, 1972)

B
(April, 1973)

Tabiklah tua..n o..oi, tabik semu..la
Dan tabik sekalian tuan oi pawang sait pawang no sedang a nya ri..mba..
Pawang menjaga tanah air bumi no, sedang
5 a bote..ra
Yang duk kawal tuan oi di bawah langit bumi no, sedang a nya ra..ta
Timur dan barat tuan oi selatan, dengan a utara..
10 Dan pada hari ini tuan oi masa ini kami nak ambil al-kesah cherita, tuan oi zaman berzaman dulu, sedang a kal ka..la
Yang jikalau salah dan silap pun nek oh, minta ampun minta maaf, semua sedang a
15 bela..ka..

Tabiklah tua..n o..oi, tabik semu..la
Dan tabik sekalian pawang sait pawang rimba, pawang menjaga tanah air, bumi bote..ra
Dan sekalian keramat aulia tuan oi zaman dulu, sedang a nya kala..
Dan pada malam inilah tuan oi kami, dan nak dengar cherita tuan oi al-kesah, zaman dulu 'ni sedang a nya ka..la
Dan kami lebih dulu persembah kepada sekalian, tok pawang sait tok pawang rimba pawang menjaga tanah air bumi, sedang a bote..ra
Yang diam di timur barat tuan oi selatan, dengan a utara..

Jangan jadi gindang ini tuan oi porak, sedang a poranda
Dan semuanya itu harap dimaaf ampun, sedang a bela..ka..
20 Apakala sudah kami memberi hormat pada sekalian aulia keramat, yang manakan a..da..
Hilang al-kesah la tuan o..i nak timbul pula, sedang a cheri..ta
25 Al-kesah tuan oi Pengkulun ni, Duli Bagi..-nda
Dan anak daripada duli.. yang mulia tuan oi, Raja Lindungan Bulan Kedah, sedang a nya Tu..a..
30 Dan raja turus negeri, zaman itu bernama tuan oi al-Marhum Maharaja kan Ja..wa
Dan permaisuri dialah yang bernama Puteri Lindung Bulan Kedah, sedang a nya Tu..a..
35 Lepas daripada itu tuan oi dia pun duduk, di dalam Lindung Bulan Kedah, sedang a nya Tu..a
Dan lebih kurang pada zaman itu tuan oi sedang a semu..la
40 Dan dapat pula seorang, sedang a bete..ra
Yang digelaran tuan oi nama Pengkulun, Duli Bagi..nda..
Kemudian ayah dan bonda itu, dan memberi diam di mahligai gading di luar, sedang a
45 kal ko..ta
Dan diberi inang pengasuh duduk kawal, serta dah ja..ga
Begitulah siang dan malam pada Pengkulun ni Duli, sedang a Bagi..nda..
50 Lepas daripada itu tuan oi pada satu hari, pada satu pula masa, sedang a semu..la
Dan duli yang mulia tadi duduk beradu di dalam, sedang a nya ko..ta
Dan besok hari, hari pun dah siang, ayam
55 pun berkokok, murai pun semua 'ni, sedang a memba..cha
Dan fajar menyingsing tuan oi merah, sedang a bernya..la
Dan duli yang mulia tadi daripada ia tidur,
60 tuan oi bangun ni selang a nya ja..ga
Dan ia pun diambil air sebatil emas, tuan oi basuh, sedang a kal mu..ka
Lepas daripada itu apakala siap sudah, ia basuh muka adat istiadat, yang manakan
65 a..da

Kiranya jikalau salah dan silap sedikit sebanyak tuan oi karangan, serta cheri..ta
Dan semuanya itu harap dimaaf ampun no, semua bela..ka..
Dan kami bertabiklah tuan oi kepada sekalian no tok pawang sait pawang rimba pawang menjaga tanah air bumi, sedang a bote..ra
Dan kerana kami, pada zaman ini nak dengar cherita tuan oi al-kesah, zaman dulu sedang a nya kala..
Dan al-kesah zaman duli, yang mulia tuan oi al-marhum, Maharaja kan Ja..wa
Yang memerentah negeri Selindung Bulan Kedah, sedang a nya Tua..
Kiranya pada zaman itu tuan oi permaisuri dialah, yang bernama tuan oi Puteri Lindung Bulan 'ni Kedah kal Tu..a
Dan anakanda pula seorang yang bernama Pengkulun, Duli Baginda..
Setelah itu pada zaman itu dia memberi diam, di luar nya ko..ta
Dan diberi inang pengasuh duduk kawal, serta nya ja..ga
Siang dan malam selamat, sedang a sejahtera..
Setelah itu tuan oi masa duli yang mulia memerentah, Selindung Bulan Kedah, sedang a nya Tu..a
Dan zaman itu tuan oi yang memerentah negeri Lindung Bulan itu, ialah yang bernama duli yang mulia tuan oi al-marhum Maharaja, sedang a nya Ja..wa..
Duduk di bawah perentah ia pada zaman itu timur barat selatan, dengan a uta..ra
Dan lebih kurang tuan oi kurang sa seratus takluk, semua bela..ka
Sehingga pada zaman itu sauk langkah sampai ke tanah, sedang a nya Ja..wa..
Tatkala ia memerentah itu tuan oi, negeri pun aman makmur, semua bela..ka
Dan saudagar pun jauh dan dekat pun banyak juga masuk keluar, tuan oi debar- ini, sedang a menia..ga..
Lepas daripada itu tuan oi hasil di dalam negeri, mas dan perak intan jema..la
Dan lembu kerbau kambing biri tuan oi, apa tah ki..ra
Dan tanam-tanaman pun pada zaman itu tuan oi subur, semua bela..ka

Dan pada waktu itu dia pun seri, sedang a bersabda
Kepada inang-inang yang manakan a..da
Dan pada pagi itu dia pun konon seri, sedang a bersabda
"Wahai inang sekalian yang manakan a..da
Dan pada hari ini, siaplah untuk santapan, sedang a kal be..ta
Adalah tujuan beta di dalam kan da..da
Dan pada hari ini beta nak mohon keluar pergi di luar, sedang a kal ko..ta
Dan hendak pergi menghadap, kepada sekalian tuan oi rakyat, sedang a jela..ta
Dan kepada sekalian orang besar-besar, sedang a nengga..ra.."
Setelah itu apakala didengar oleh inang pengasuh, da..n dengar bersabda daripada titah perentah, tuan oi duli amat sedang a muli..a
Dan mereka itu pun kalang kabutlah, dengan a semu..la
Siapkan hidangan, sedang a semu..la
Dan untuk santapan tuan oi duli yang amat, sedang a muli..a

Dan riuh dan rendah gegak gempi..ta
Dan serta merta tuan oi rakyat, sedang a jela..ta..
Adalah pada satu hari pula, maka duli yang mulia tadi duduk beradu, di dalam a nya ko..ta
Dan besok hari, hari pun dah siang no, ayam pun berkokok, murai pun semua 'ni sedang a memba..cha
Dan fajar menyingsinglah tuan o..oi, merah bernyala..
Dan setelah itu tuan oi duli yang mulia tadi pun daripada ia beradu, sedang dia pun bangun, akan a nya ja..ga
Dan ia pun diambil air sebatil mas, lalu dibasuh, sedang a kal mu..ka
Apakala dia pun basuh muka siap semua, habis a bela..ka
Dan setelah itu dia pun bertitah, sambil berka..ta
Dan kepada inang pengasuh, yang manakan ada..
Setelah itu dia pun telah bersabda kepada inang, sedang a nya tu..a
Dan ia pu..n suruh tuan oi lengkaplah, hidang-hidangan untuk santapan, sedang a di ra..ja
Setelah itu apakala didengar, oleh inang pengasuh, yang manakan a..da
Dan santapan di raja itu pun dia pun kalang kabut tuan oi disiap, sedang a semu..la

Pr. 2. Haji Isahak bin Daud, Arau, Perlis. ± 85

MALIM DEMAN

A

(Oct. 1963)

Ada satu konon, ada satu chetera, zaman tatkala sedang dulu.. kala...
Raja bernama Tengku Si Malim Dewa, permaisuri nama Tengku Si Mala..m Bongsu...
Negeri bernama Pagar Riung Payu..ng Sekaki...
Tengku Si Malim Dewa memangku empat puluh tahun menjadi raja, tak mahu boleh anak denga..n putera, berapa disait berapa

B

(April, 1973)

Ada satu konon, ada satu chetera, sedang tatkala zama..n dulukala..
Raja nama lo Tengku Si Malim Dewa, negeri bernama Pagar Riu..ng Payung Sekaki..
Permaisuri nama Tengku.. Si Malam Bongsu..
Berapa diniat berapa dikait berapa kenduri segala alim pendita, tak mahu boleh anak denga..n putera..

dikait, berapa disait berapa diniat segala alim pendita, segala fakir hina dina, fakir miskin, semua niat kai..t belaka, minta do'a bole..h putera...

15 Yang berkat orang fakir yang alim fakir yang miskin, segala alim pendita, mengandunglah, Tengku Si Mala..m Bongsu...

Mengandung tujuh bulan mengandung panggil, bidan tujuh bidan ketiga, rasa
20 tengok sebenar a- mengandu..ng putera...

Bidan tujuh bidan ketiga berhimpun, rumah- a- di balai peseban agu..ng-, di balai peseban agu..ng-, balai Tengku Si Mali..m Dewa...

25 Bidan tujuh bidan ketiga, angkit tangan menyusun atas kepala, "Ampun tuanku batu kepala, nak rasa perut Tengku Si Mala..m Bongsu..."

Rasa perut masing-masing rasa belaka,
30 sebenarlah bunting tujuh bulan Tengku.. Si Malam Bongsu...

Bunting Tengku Malam Bongsu panggil pula nujum nerus panggil, tujuh orang buka nerus yang ketika, nak tengok atau laki-laki
35 atau perempua..nlah juga...

Hulubalang pahlawan panggil "Nujum nerus nujum ketika 'engan segera, di balai peseba..n agu..ng

Sampai di balai peseban agung Tengku Si
40 Malim Dewa pun panggil, "Nujum nerus nujum nujum ketiga, buka nerus denga..n ketika...

Buka nerus dengan ketika hei nujum, 'chu tengok anak, anak dia laki-laki atau
45 perempua..nlah juga..."

Nujum masing-masing buka nerus ketika, semua masing-masing tengok semua dalam nerus ketika, kuling-kuling kepala, angkit tangan, "Ampun tuanku beribu ampun,"
50 angkit tangan, tujuh orang menyusun atas kepala, "Jika karam tak berayar bakar tak berapi gantung tak bertali, kalau tak silap paham patik anak tuanku 'ni, perempua..n juga..."

55 Raja Tengku Malim Dewa pun sukalah tak kira-kira, kenduri segala alim pendita, pakir yang miskin, suka nak bole..h putera...

Chukup genap sembilan bulan lo meng-
60 andung, Tengku Si Malam Bongsu mengandung, chukup genap sembilan bulan, sakitlah

Tak boleh anak dengan putera, berapa disait berapa di- sait, berapa dikenduri segala orang tua-tua, segala orang dulu kala, minta boleh anak denga..n putera..

Ada satu masa, sedang tatkala lo sekenduri segala, orang alim pendita, boleh mengandung anak Tengku.. Si Malam Dewi, sukalah Raja Malim Bongsu dengan Tengku.. Si Malim Dewa..

Berapa diseronok berapa diramai apa disait dikait, segala alim pendita, kendur kendara, riuh rendah, dalam negeri Payu..n Sekaki..

Mengandunglah Tengku Malim Dewi, lebih kurang tiga bulan denga..n dua..

Panggil segala alim pendita kenduri kendara segala alim ulama, Tengku Si Malim Dewa mengandung Tengku.. Si Malim Dewi..

Permaisuri bernama Tengku.. Si Malam Bongsu..

Duduk lama tak lama chukup genaplah Che' Na.., sampai masa, sampailah bula..n, mengandung sembilan bulan, Tengku.. Si Malim Dewi... a- Malam Bongsu...

Mengandung lo berapa suka segala rakyat bala segala pengasuh mak sahaya hamba sahaya seronok ramai di tanah tid- e- di tanah atas rumah, segala pengasuh mak inang dayang-dayang, segala bida..n pengasuh, segala bidan semua, mak bidan ketujuh bidan- bidan ketujuh bidan ketiga, semua berhimpun belaka, siap segala latikar lampin adat istiadat orang tua-tua, semenaja..k zaman dulu kala...

Duduk tak berapa lama chukup genap sampai bulan Tengku Si Malam Bongsu sampai bulan, mebunyilah pula guruh lintar segala ribut topan, nak petera Tengku.. Si Malam Dewi.., segala lintar guruh topan bunyi, nak putera Tengku.. Si Malim Dewi..

Ramai segala segala pengasuh mak inang hamba sahaya riuh rendah atas rumah, di atas- di bawah ada belaka, terhimpun nak putera Tengku.. Si Malim Dewi...

Segala ribut topan heran habis segala rakyat bala, apa pedah 'tu peturun ribut topan, segala lintar guruh semua ada belaka, nak putera- nak putera Tengku.. Si Malim Dewi...

panggil pula bidan tujuh bidan ketiga, riuh rendah di dalam kota...

65 Bidan tujuh bidan ketiga, riuh rendah di dalam kota, empat belas haribulan kembang chuacha, hari Jumaa..tlah juga...

Segala rakyat bala suka, tak mereta empat belas haribulan kembang chuacha, suka ramai dayang pengasuh inang dalam, kota
70 Pagar Riung Payu..ng Sekaki...

Ayam berkokok murai membacha, fajar menyingsing atas kepala, ada satu lo guruh la- guruh lintarlah bunyi, daamat di dalam, negeri Pagar, Riung Payu..ng Sekaki...

75 Heranlah masing-masing ribut topan guruh lintar, apa pedah dengan pestaka, yang jadi demikian 'ni, tak pernah dengar lagi.. demikian 'ni...

Habis topan meneru guruh lintar pun
80 habis kembang chuacha, Tuan Puteri Malam Bongsu pun sudah kelua..r putera...

(Recording by *Dewan Bahasa*)

Segala bidan pengasuh mak inang pun duk susun ayam berkokok murai membacha fajar menyingsing di atas kepala, puteralah Tengku.. Si Malim Dewi..

Anak perempuan sukalah Raja Malim Dewa, segala pengasuh mak inang hamba sahaya, datuk menteri hulubalang semua terhimpu..nlah belaka...

Segala datuk me- datuk temenggung hulubalang, suka belaka Tengku Malim Dewa pun, ramai suka ria tak kira-kira, tak pernah boleh anak dengan putera, umur empat puluh tahun tak boleh anak denga..n putera...

Seronok ramai segala pengasuh mak inang hamba sahaya bidan semua bidan tujuh bidan ketiga semua ada semua belaka.., seperti adat raja-raja zaman dulu.. kala...

Duduk sejulung sejenang berdengan dua, sait dikait panggil segala datuk menteri hulubalang nak kenduri kendara, suka Tengku Si Malim Dewa boleh anak, putera Si Malim- Tengku Si Mali..m Dewi, bonda bernama Tengku.. Si Malam Bongsu...

C

(April, 1972)

Ada satu konon lo ei, ada satu chetera, sedang tatkala zaman dulu.. kala...

Raja bernama lo Tengku Si Malim Dewa, permaisuri nama Tengku Si Malam
5 Bongsu...

Lama tak lama Raja- Malim Dewa tak mahu boleh anak denga..n putera...

Berapa disait berapa dikait, segala ali..m ulama...

10 Dengan berkat lo alim bernama, mengandunglah Tengku Si Mala..m Bongsu...

Mengandung lo anak yang perempuan nama Tengku Si Malam Dewi...

Sukalah raja segala rakyat bala hamba
15 sahaya, laung di tanah di- e-, laung di atas rumah di tana..h menyahut, suka.., Raja Tengku Si Malam Dewa, dengan Tengku.. Si Malam Bongsu...

Duduk lu lama tak berapa lama, lebih
20 kurang tiga tahun denga..n dua...

Mengandung pula beran- mengandung pula oh Tengku Si Mali..m Dema..n .....

Pr. 3. Mahmud bin Wahid, Mata Air, Perlis. ± 70

AWANG BELANGA

A
(March, 1972)

He..i, ayo salam, Mak Munah, a Che' Likun, mengunjung tabik, kami 'ngunjung, che' semba..h

He..i, telah sudah, a che' makan, ah oh
5 pinang, makan sepiak, dua tiga, a menolak, a che' suda..h

He..i, .., ayo salam, Mak Munah, a Che' Likun, jawat salam, 'ngunjung tabik, kami 'ngunjung, che' semba..h

10 He..i, pada tuan kampung, tuan rumah, tuan yang pimpin, jemput kami mari, .., pada 'tika 'ni, pada waktu 'ni, pada nga jam, che' nga 'ni..

He..i, a riuh dan rendah, oh gegak,
15 gemita, taada dah nga apa, nak 'ngambil, che' kata..

He..i, hang tengok aku, aku tengok hang, .., hang gelak 'kat aku, aku kenyeh, 'kat nga ha..ng

20 He..i, hang kejit mata, aku kenyut misai, .., riuh rendah, pakat tengok, Awang pula, hai Belanga..

He..i, habis tabik, pada tuan rumah, tuan kampung, .., pada ketua kita, a di sini,
25 tabik-tabiklah semua, .., mana tak kena, pakat tolong, pekena, mana tak betul, pakat tolong, perbetu..l

He..i, timbul che' kesah, tabik keramat, a di sini, yang pegang, tanah ng ayar, api ng
30 angin, che' sini..

He..i, daripada keramat, Kedah .., adik Kak Chik Kak Chak, Mak Long Mak Ngah, .., tabik-tabik semua, .., mana dah ng ada, pada 'tika, che' nga 'ni..

35 He..i, timbul che' kesah, pula tabik, a jin tanah, jembalang bumi, mangku bumi, a di pusat, e che' bumi..

He..i, nga jin dah hitam, pula nga jin, che' putih, nga jin dan hijau, menyala, ke
40 langi..t

He..i, habis tabik, pada tuan kampung, tuan rumah, ketua kita, pada keramat, pada nga jin, tabik-tabik semua, .., timbul che' pula, guru tua, a 'ni guru, che' muda..

B
(April, 1972)

He...ei, telah sudah, a che' makan, a oh pinang, makan sepiak, dua tiga, a menolak, a che' suda..h

He..ei, .., dua tiga, menolak, a che' sudah, ayo salam, Mak Munah, a Che' Liku..n

He..i, mengunjung tabik, mengunjung sembah, .., pada tuan kampung, tuan rumah, tuan kechil, a oh besar, tua muda, jantan-jantan betina, tabik-tabiklah semua, .., tuan memimpin, a yang jemput, 'ni kami, che' mai..n

Hei...ei, .., ala habis tabik, kechil besar, tua muda, jantan betina, Mak Long Mak Ngah, Kak Chik Kak Chak, tabik-tabiklah semua, .., mana tak kena, pakat tolong, pekena, mana tak betul, pakat tolong, perbetu..l

He...ei, .., pada 'tika 'ni, waktu nga 'ni, a riuh rendah, di gegak, gemita..

He..i, taada dah siapa, nak 'ngambil, che' kata, hang tengok aku, aku tengok hang, hang gelak 'kat aku, aku kenyeh, 'kat nga ha..ng

He..ei, hang kesot mai, aku kesot pi, .., hang pegang ng aku, aku pegang, che' nga ha..ng

He..i, riuh ramai, pakat dengar, pula nga Awang, Belanga..

He...ei, .., ramai di kampung, kami tabik, a di kampung, ramai di padang, che' tabik, a di pada..ng

He..i, nga jin dah tanah, jembalang, a oh bumi, mangku dah bumi, di pusat, a che' bumi..

He..i, nga jin dah hitam, sedang dah jin putih, jin hijau, pula menyala, ke langi..t

He..i, guru dah tua, pula guru, oh muda, .. ai guru, mu..da, kami salin, tok guru..

He..i, bukan dah main, kami tiru, meniru, ka..ami, duk turun, pula baris, yang dulu..

He..i, habis tabik, segala, tuan kampung, tuan rumah, tuan yang pimpin, kami main, tabik-tabik juga, .., habis tabik, guru tua,

45 He..i, guru muda, kami duk salin, lah oh guru, ada dah dulu, 'ni nga ada, dah sekara..ng
He..i, ada dah dulu, ada pula, a sekarang, bukan dah main, kami tiru, meniru..
50 He..i, bukan dah main, pula tiru, meniru, .. eh kami, duk turun, pula baris, yang dulu..
He..i, habis tabik, pada guru tua, guru muda, .., pulang pulih, sedia kala, pulang
55 tuan, pusat tasik, a pauh janggi, sena rendang, sana tuan, beradu...
He....ei, hilang royat, a berita, nak timbul, timbul tersebut, che ng Awang, Belanga..
60 He..i, hilang tersebut, pula timbul, bernama, sebuah negeri, Raja Radin, sangat .., 'ni zalim, buat pula, atas hamba, che' rakya..t
He..i, ada pada, suatu masa, .., timbul
65 kesah, Mek Siti Galin, hak ng orang, masakin, chari pagi, a duk makan, che' pagi..
He..i, chari petang, duk makan, che' peta..ng
70 He..i, tiap-tiap hari, tiap-tiap pula, dia hidup, duk chari kayu, ng api, tukar beras, boleh makan, a 'ni tukar, a che' maka..n,
He..i, ada pada, suatu masa, .., masuk rimba, chari kayu, lapar dahaga, oi ng ayar,
75 tuju di sana, tuju sini, dalam hutan rimba, chari ng ayar, tak jumpa, a che' lagi.
He..i, jalan nga pi, jalan nga mai, turun di katur, tengok pula, ayar dalam katur, oi ng ada, dalam tapak, 'ni gajah, che'
80 gaja..h
He..i, Mek Siti Galin, tunduk-tunduk, hirup ng ayar, dia makan, semulut, sampai kenyang, hilang dahaga, .., hilang lapar, sudah dia mai, dia pula, ambil kayu, berkas
85 kayu, dia junjung, bawa bali..k
He..i, telah sudah, dia balik, oi kayu, ayun temayun, sampai ke rumah, .., matahari jatuh, gelap gulita, sudah malam, che' hari..
90 He..i, sudah malam, pun hari, dia chapai, oh timba, tuju telaga, .., ambil ng ayar, a naik atas rumah, .., chapai periuk, basuh beras, lengkap pula, nasi 'ni, makanan chukup, dia seorang, a che' diri..
95 He..i, sudah masak, a oh nasi, .., dia ng angkit, makan minum, telah sudah, makan guru muda, ramai sini, yang pegang, tanah ng ayar, api ng angin, che' sini..

He...ei, .., pulang pulih, a sedia, che' kala, pulanglah tuan, .., pusat tasik, pauh janggi, sena rendang, sana tuan, beradu..

He...ei, .., hilang royat, a berita, nak timbul, timbul pula, .. tersebut, che nga Awang, Belanga..

He..i, sudah tersebut, eh sebuah, negeri, raja bernama, .., Raja Radin, a merentah, dalam negeri, dari muda, sampai ke tu- eh, che' tua..

He..i, sebut dah kesah, Raja Radin, sangat zalim, atas hamba rakyat, .., hukum hakam, merentah, ha negeri..

He..i, hilanglah kesah, pula Raja, oi Radin, timbul dah kesah, Mek Siti Galin, .., masakin sangat, chari pagi, duk makan, che' pagi, chari dah petang, duk makan, che' peta..ng

He..i, Mek Siti Galin, duduk pula, dalam negeri, Raja Radin, a che' tadi, chari makan, hulu negeri, 'ni hilir, negeri..

He..i, ada pada, ada waktu, che' masa, Mek Siti Galin, .., pergi pula, a ke rimba, chari kayu ng api, nak bawa, balik jual, di kampu..ng

He..i, tiap-tiap hari, tiap-tiap bulan, juga begitu, chari kayu, duk tukar beras, dimakan, pula dia, oi hidup, di situ..

He..i, ada pada, sewaktu, che' hari, dia nga pi ng hutan, .., lapar dahaga, dalam rimba, chari ng ayar, makan ng ayar, chari sana, sini pula, tak dapa..t

He..i, chari sana, chari sini, lama-lama, turun dalam katur, .., dia pandang, ada ng ayar, dalam lopak, a che' gaja..h

He..i, dia pergi, tepi lopak, dia ng ambil, oh ng ayar, sua tangan, dia ambil hirup, dia minum, hilang lapar, a dahaga, che' ng aya..r

He..i, telah sudah, hilang dahaga, lapar ng ayar, dia chapai kayu, .., berkas kayu, dia junjung, a berjalan, pula .., dalam rimba, habis rimba, pula terus, ke pada..ng

He..i, telah sudah, sampai pula, ke padang, habis padang, masuk kampung, .., habis kampung, habis padang, baru sampai, pula rumah, a che' dia..

He..i, sampai-sampai, ke rumah, matahari pun, sudah petang, ayun temayun, .., dia pun chapai, a oh timba, tuju telaga, ng

nasi, .., malam pun sudah, nak jauh hari, dia mai duk, di rumah, makan pinang, se ng orang, a che' diri..
100 He..i, telah sudah, makan pinang, sudah jauh hari, tengah malam, .., dia pun masuk, dalam bilik, padam lampu, dia terus, che' lena..
He..i, tengah lena, ayam pun kokok,
105 jarang-jarang basa, murai 'mbacha, di luar pagar, fajar menyingsing, merah nyala, panas penuh padang, siang hari, che' pula..

ambil ng ayar, hela baru naik, a di ng atas, che' ruma..h
He..i, telah sudah, naik ke rumah, chapai beras, bubuh periuk, dia siap, .., lengkap man-, makan minum, semua chukup, a che' lengka..p
He..i, matahari pun, sudah malam, gelap gulita, dia masak, oh nasi, angkit nasi, pula makan, che' nasi..
He..i, telah sudah, makan nasi, tengah sudah jauh, oi hari, jauh malam, dia duduk, di ibu rumah, seorang diri, ayam a pun, sudah dekat, nak kokok, melengung pi, fikir nga mai, han chari, che' maka..n
He..i, habis fikir, dia masuk, dalam bilik, padam lampu, dia terus, che' lena..
He..i, telah sudah, dia lena, ayam pun kokok, jarang-jarang basa, murai 'mbacha, keluar pagar, fajar menyingsing, .., panas penuh padang, merah nyala, siang hari, che' bali..k

Fadhil, Langkawi.

AWANG BELANGA

He...ei..ei..ei....
tersebut pula, satu cherita, .., raja dalam, negeri itu, perempuan dia, lah hamil, mengida..m, nak makan, daging pelandu..k, lah puti...h

Hei...ei..ei..ei....
telah ng itu, raja pun, suruh orang, memukul chanang, .., apabila, dengar chanang, rakyat bala, datanglah ke, rumah raja, orang yang chapik, datang bertongkat, yang pekak, leka bertanya, dah ditanya, sepatah sekali, jadi dua, sepatah dua, jadi tiga, dah ditanya, ditanya ditanya-tanya-tanya-tanya-tanya, ditanya juga..

Hei...ei..ei..ei....
lalu kata, nya raja, .., "Adalah, beta suruh, orang pukul, lah chanang, bagi tahu, semua .., .., semua rakyat, nya beta, hajat beta, tidak dua, tidak tiga, nak suruh pergi, memburu, hujung negeri, chari pelanduk putih, perempuan beta, .., isteri beta, mengidam nak makan, daging, pelanduk puti...h."

He...ei..ei..ei....
setelah ng itu, setelah ng itu, jalanlah, .., orang yang, nak pergi, memburu, pelanduk putih, tok pawang, jalan dulu, yang lain, ikut di belakang, .., lama lama, tak berapa lama, masuk hutan, keluar hutan, sampailah, hujung negeri...

Hei...ei..ei..ei....
tersebut pula, satu cherita, sebut pula, satu cherita, tok pawang tadi, lalu jumpa, dengan Mak, Siti Galin, .., lalu kata, tok pawang, .., "Chuba tengok, orang perempuan, mari mana, duduk sini, hujung negeri, seorang diri..."

Hei..ei..ei..ei....
lalu kata, Mak Siti Galin, .., "Asal mak, orang kayangan, jatuh ke dunia, duk melarat, atas negeri, inilah dia, mak duduk, huju..ng, nege..ri, krrrr

(Recording by Datuk Syed Idrus, Alor Setar)

Kd.1. **Abdullah Omar bin Ismail**, Kampung Belantik, Sik, Kedah. ±50

JUBANG LINGGANG

A
(March, 1972)

Ayo baatera lama tu-denga..n wei lama.. ga' ei...

Ayo pelapik timang pelapung bari bari ga' terbang be...ei deru.. terbang hinggap
5 Kuala Terbang

Minta suruh tabik tuan di kampung hamba nak chetera hikayat bari jaman da..wei dulu ada dulu ada se..karang

Nak royat satu royat satu chetera satu
10 buah negeri

Negeri bernama negeri Tanjung Luluk Kuala Air Mulih Jambatan nga Emas Tebing Berukir Awang Bersanggit Matahari Lima Chempaka Berapit Chermai
15 Rendang ga' Buding Be...wei..rem..as Sena Sejajar

Tempat anak punai gading naik me..niti.. wei daha..n

Rajanya bernama Tok Raja Besa..r
20 menterinya bernama Tuan Puteri Mayang Buih

Dua beradik 'ngan Tuan Puteri Ratna.. wei Bongsu..

Anaknya kakak Timang Gading Joba..ng,
25 adiknya Timang Gading Linggang, duk berhenti Jong Baluk Gendang Galai Lalu Api ng Asal

Di Teluk Tujuh Pantai Sembilan Hujung Tanjung Olak Pulau Lima Pasir Debu
30 Mayang Me..ngurai

Di Pantai Gelenggang tempat kechau berseruling remis bersiul lokan bertepuk udang udang me..wei..nari..

Di susur kolam berpagarkan buluh
35 perindu kolam bertajuk ga' buding be.. wei..remas, di kaki.. Gunu..ng wei Bayu..

Dia duk nanti hari dengan ketika.. dia nak kundang ke punchak Gunu..ng wei..

B
(April, 1973)

Ayo baatera lama tu-denga..n wei lama.. ga' ei.. ayo pelapik timang pelapung baribari ga' terbang be..wei..deru..

Terbang hinggap Kuala Talubang minta suruh tabik tuan di kampung hamba nak chetera hikayat raja bari jaman da..wei dulu...

Ada dulu ada sekara..ng nak timbul satu royat satu chetera satu buah negeri

Negeri bernama negeri Tanjung Luluk Kuala Air Mulih Jambatan nga Emas Tebing Berukir Awang Bersanggit Matahari Lima Chempaka Berapit Chermai Rendang ga' Buding Be..re.wei.rema..s Sena Sejajar tempat anak punai gading naik me..niti.. wei daha..n

Rajanya bernama Tok Raja Besa..r menterinya bernama Tuan Puteri Mayang Buih

Dua beradik 'ngan Tuan Puteri Ratna.. wei Bongsu.. Dia duk di Tan- negeri Tanjung Luluk

Anaknya kakak Timang Gading Joba..ng, adiknya Timang Gading Linggang dia duk berhenti letih berhenti lengah

Diberi nama kata di muka kua..la negeri Pasi..r wei Maya..ng

Dia sudah gi bersintuk berlimau di Pulau Mendung Pulau Lima Pulau Sembilan ga' Pulau Se..wei..jempu..ng

Bertentang 'ngan muka kua..la negeri Pas..ir wei Maya..ng

Dia duk nanti hari nanti ketika.. dia nak kundang ke punchak Gunu..ng wei Bayu..

Dia duk bersiap bersimpan sudah siaplah dia..

Dia pun taapalah dia Timang Gading Jobang pun dia duk tarik ke layar naik

Bayu.. duk berhenti letih berhenti lengah
40 Dia pun taapalah dia duk berhenti sejulung sejenang lama tiga hari tiga malam
Tujuh hari tujuh malam lama dia duk nantilah dia pun lagi, nak kundang ke punchak Gunu..ng wei Bayu...
45 Lama Timang Gading Jobang pun di hati sudah duk melembung-lembung ke punchak Gunung Bayu
Duk ng ingat ke ng adik Tuan Puteri Kuntum Delima dua beradik dengan Tuan
50 Puteri Kesumba.. wei Muru..p
Dia pun taapalah dia bingkas bangun di tiang 'gong tiang gambang dia.. menujulah dia ke bilik kurung adik dia Timang Gadi..ng wei Lengga..ng
55 Dia duk buka pintu bilik adik dia duk menggerak "Ng adi..k ayo wei adik kepada ng abang
Adik jangan duk lerah tikar segulung wei adik ga' bantal se..wei..lipa..t ke mana-
60 mana kita jalana..n a wei jau..h"
Dia pun duk gerak adik dia gerak ke kiri ga' balik ke..wei.. kana..n gerak ke kanan balik ke.. kiri
Lama-lama ayo wei ng aba..ng dia
65 Timang Gading Lenggang pun dia chelek mata tengok abang duk me..nangis jatuh air mata ga' tajun me..wei..naju..n
Dia pun lagi "Baapa wei ng aba..ng siapa hambat abang la ng abang siapa halau ng
70 abang siapa palu.. wei ng aba..ng?"
"Ayo la ng adi..k abang la ng adik
Tak boleh lama tak boleh duduk wei adik di Teluk Tujuh Pantai Sembila..n hati sudah duk melembung-lembung naik ke
75 punchak Gunung Bayu
Duk ng ingatkan adik Tuan Puteri Kuntum Delima dua beradik 'ngan Tuan Puteri Kesumba.. wei Muru..p."

Dia simpan tali bubut tali temberang kelat layar topang China di.. wei lau..t
Sudah siap adik dia Timang Gading Linggang pun dia gi duk berdiri di tiang 'gong tiang gambang
Duk berdiri ke kaki tunggal lenggak ke langit awan berkisar tunduk ke bumi bumi me..wei.lengga..ng
Tunduk ke laut air menyepak ke timur a wei rua..ng
Dia pun bersaksilah dia sedang "Ya Allah ya Tuhanku Rabi dulu Allah kemudian jadi
Sungguh bertuah aku lagi berdiri sakti aku anak chuchu chichit Tok Mengkadung Sakti yang bertulang tunggal
Bulu roma sungsang berair-liur masin berdarah putih berlida..h wei ng hita..m turun ke ng aku bertambah lebih
Aku nak minta berturun angin sarang saring angin di langit angin kuntum bunga angin kisara..n wei payu..ng

Kd.2. **Had bin Mat Arif**, Ulu Tawar, Kedah. ±60

RAJA LOTONG

A
(6th April, 1972)

Oh oh o..h nik o..h minta wei tabik,
ng ora..ng ke-
ramat sangat lagi.., tu-da..ri
sini jangan seora..ng, menga..mbil

B
(6th April, 1972)

Oh oh o..h nik o..h minta wei tabik,
ng ora..ng ke-
ei ramat sangat lagi.., tu-da..ri
ei sini tabik seora..ng, tab..ik se-

5   ei salah jangan seora..ng, menga..bil
    ei silih kaum kerama..t, sepua..k ke-
    ei ramat tabik seora..ng, tab..ik se-
    mua tabik empat bedaha..p, peju..ru
    alam tujuh jeru..ng, jong lapan wei..
10 timang deksa nik der, ayo denda..ng
    che' donda..ng di.., eh dondang.

    Oh oh o..h nik o..h lepas be..remas,
    bere..mas
    pula emas semaya..ng, dala..m che-
15 rana lepas bermaaf, berma..af
    ah pula maaf seora..ng, maaf wei...
    timang semua nik der, ayo denda..ng
    che' donda..ng di..., di dondang.

    Oh oh o..h nik o..h balas wei..ng
20 hamba, mene..bas
    bikung buat saja..k, ke te..ngah
    ng uma balas ng hamba, mena..rik
    lotong buat saja..k, ayo tidak wei...
    timang kena nik der, ayo denda..ng
25 che' donda..ng di.., di dondang

    Oh (c)
    Oh oh o..h nik o..h hilang wei..
    royat, hila..ng che-
    rita timbul tersebu..t, nga ma..
30 nga..Mak
    ei Sekin keluar terbi..t, di da..lam
    ng anjun..g 'nuju pula.., jemu..ran
    ei besar jemuran buju..r, jemuran wei..
    timang lentang nik der, ayo denda..ng
35 che' donda..ng di.., di dondang

    Oh oh o..h nik o..h lalu wei..pula,
    nga ma..Mak
    ei Seki..n nampak terpanda..ng, ke
    pa..rang
40 puti..ng, nga ma...Mak
    ei Sekin (c) chapai pula.. ke pa..rang
    ai puti...ng, nga ma..Mak
    ei Sekin hendak nak chari.., ke ka..yu
    ng api (c)
45 jalan wei.. belang, nga ma..Mak
    ai Sekin berjalan bela..ng, mele..nggang
    ei belang menuju pula.., belu..kar
    ei muda belukar muda.., belu..kar
    ei tua sangat lama.., seju..lung
50 lama dua kali.., bertu..juh
    hari dua kali.., bertu..juh
    malam duk chari.., ke ka..yu
    api habis pula.., sesat wei..
    timang belarat nik der, ayo denda..ng
55 che' donda..ng di.., ga' di dondang

ei mua (c) tabik seora..ng, tabi..k se-
ei mua tabik tida..k, menye..but
nama tabik tida..k, berta..ting
ei nama kaum seora..ng, kau..m semua empat bedaha..p, peju..ru
alam tujuh jeru..ng, jong lapan wei...
timang deksa nik der, ayo denda..ng
che' donda..ng di.., di dondang

Oh oh o..h nik o..h lepas be..remas,
bere..mas
pula emas semaya..ng. dala..m che-
ei rana lepas berma..af, berma..af
pula maaf seora..ng, maaf wei...
timang semua nik der, ayo denda..ng
che' donda..ng di.., di dondang

Oh oh o..h nik o..h wei balas wei..ng
hamba, mene..bas
bikung buat saja..k, ke te..ngah
ng uma balas ng hamba.., mena..rik
lotong buat saja..k, ayo tidak wei...
timang kena nik der, ayo denda..ng
che' donda..ng di.., ga' di dondang

Oh oh o..h nik o..h hila..ng wei..royat,
hila..ng che-
rita nga ma..Mak
ei Sekin keluar terbit, di da..lam
ei ng anju.ng a na- (c)   menuju pula..,
jemu..ran
ei besar jemuran buju..r, jemu..ran
ah lentang nampak terpanda..ng, ke
pa..rang
puti...ng, ng ma..Mak
ei Sekin

Oh oh o..h nik o..h lalu wei..pula, nga
ma..Mak
ei Sekin chapai pula.. ke pa..rang
ei puting hendak nak chari.., ke ka..yu
ng api.., nga ma..Mak
ei Sekin

Oh oh o..h nik o..h jalan (c)
Oh oh o..h nik o..h lalu.. wei pula,
ng ma..Mak
ai Sekin chapai pula, ke para..ng
puting hendak nak chari.., ke ka..yu
ng api belenggang belang (c) menuju
pula-menuju pula.., belu..kar
ei muda belukar muda.., belu..kar
ei tua sangat duk chari.., ke ka..yu
ng api sangat lama.., seju..lung
lama habis pula.., sesat wei..:
timang berlarat nik der, ayo denda..ng

Oh oh o..h nik o..h lalu wei.. pula,
ng ma..Mak
ei Sekin duk chari.., ke ka..yu
ng api sampai pula.., ke te..ngah
ei rimba matahari pula.. di su..dah
60 lohor... (etc.)

che' donda..ng di.., ga' di dondang

Oh oh o..h nik o..h jalan wei.. belang,
nga ma..Mak
ei Sekin jalan belang, melengga..ng
ei belang ga' dia duk chari.., ke ka..yu
oh ng api sangat lama.., sejulu..ng
oh lama sampai pula.., ke te..ngah
ei rimba matahari pula.., di su..dah
lohor... (etc.)

Kd.3. Had bin Mat Arif.

JUBANG LINGGANG

A
(June, 1966)

B
(April, 1972)

Oh o..h nik o..h
kejut wei.. jaga, Tok Ra..ja..
ei Besar kejut jaga.., lada di..
tidu..r, Tok Ra..ja
5 ei Besar keluar terbi..t, di ba..lai
ei di besar jawab bole..h, Tok Ra..ja
ei Besar.

"Ayu wei.. kundang, kepa..da
ei ng hamba ng ambil pula.., ke ja..la
10 ei kechil jala kechi..l, ke ja..la
ei besar kita gi champa..k, ke pa..ntai
'ni nga laut kalau nak kena.., ke ng
  a..na..k
'ni ga' ikan."

15 Oh oh o..h nik o..h
berjala..n wei.. belang, me..le..nggang
ei belang (c) ga' lagi.., Tok Ra..ja
ei Besar berjalan bela..ng, mele..nggang
ei belang dengan pula.., si ku..ndang
20 ei dia menuju pula.., ke pa..ntai
ei nga laut sangat lama.., seju..lung
'ni lama dua kali.., bertu..juh
ah hari dua kali.., bertu..juh
ei malam sampai pula.., ke pa..ntai
25 'ni ga' nga laut.

Oh oh o..h nik o..h
lalu.. wei.. pula, Tok Ra..ja
ei Besar chapai pula.., ke ja..la
ei besar jala besa..r, si pa..nja..ng
30 'ni ga' tujuh.

Oh oh o..h nik o..h
champak wei.. pula, Tok Ra..ja
ei Besar nga duk champa..k, ke ja..la

Oh o..h nik o..h
hilang wei.. royat, hila..ng cherita timbul tersebu..t, Tok Ra..ja
ei Besar duduk menyeta..k, di ba..lai
ei besar jawab bole..h, Tok Ra..ja
ei Besar.

"Ayu wei.. kundang, kepa..da
ei hamba ambil pula.., si ja..la
ei besar jala besa..r, si ja..la
ei kechi..l jalai be- jala besa..r, si
  pa..njang
ei tubuh ki- (c) si pa..njang
ei tuju..h kita berjala.., ke pantai wei..
timang laut nik- (c)
kita berjala.., 'kut pa..ntai..
'ni ga' nga laut."

Oh oh o..h nik o..h
lalu.. wei.. kundang, si cha..pai..
'ni pula sangat lagi.., ke ja..la..
ei besar jala besa..r, si ja..la..
ei kechil (c) jala besa..r, si ja..la..
ei kechil menuju pula.., ke pa..ntai..
laut dengan (c) menuju pula.., ke pa..ntai..
ei laut.

Oh oh o..h nik o..h
lalu.. wei.. pula, Tok Ra..ja..
ei Besar chapai pula.., ke ja..la..
ei besar duduk champa..k, ke ja..la..
ei besar sangat (c) sangat lagi..,
  ke pa..ntai..
laut sangat lama.., seju..lung
lama jawab bole:.h, Tok Ra..ja..
ei Besar.

ei besar champak ke kiri.., champa..k ke
35 ei kanan sangat lama.., seju..lung
'ni lama jawab bole..h, Tok Ra..ja
ei Besar "Ng ayo kunda..ng, kepa..da
ei hamba apa bala.., denga..n che-
ei taka kita champa..k, ke ja..la
40 ei besar nga duk champa..k, ke pa..ntai
ei nga laut jangan lagi.., ke nga a..nak
ah ng ikan sampah pula.., tia..da
ah lekat sangat lagi.., ke ja..la
ei kita sial dimana.., maja..l di..
45 'ni ga' mana?"

Oh oh o..h nik o..h
wei kund..ang wei.. pula, di cha..pai
ei pula.., ke ja..la
ei kechil ng duk champa..k, ke ja..la
50 ei kechil champak ke kiri.., champak (c)
champak ke kiri.., champa..k ke
ei kanan jawab bole..h, tu-de..ngan
"Ei kundang ambuh nga ma..k, ambu..h ke
ei tuan apa bala.., denga..n che-
55 ei taka aku duk champa..k ke ja..la
ei kechil jangan lagi.., ke nga a..nak
ei ikan sampah pula.., tia..da
ei lekat sangat lagi.., ke ja..la..
'ni ga' kita."

60 Oh oh o..h nik o..h
jawab wei.. bole..h, Tok Ra..ja
ei Besar "Ng ayo kunda..ng, kepa..da
ei (c) hamba kita gi champa..k, di lu..buk
ei besa..r lubuk besa..r, ke ba..tu..
65 'ni ga' besar."

Oh oh o..h nik o..h
jalan wei.. bela..ng, mele..nggang
ei belang sangat lagi.., Tok Ra..ja
ei Besar menuju pula.., ke lu..bu..k
70 'ni ga' besar.

Oh oh o..h nik o..h
sampai wei.. pula.. 'ni ke lu..buk
ei di besar nga duk champa..k, ke ja..la
ei besar jala besa..r, si pa..njang
75 ei tubu..h nampak pula.., ke pu..chu..k
'ni ga' jala.

Oh oh o..h nik o..h
tarik wei.. pula, Tok Ra..ja
ei Besar tarik pula.., ke ja..la
80 ei besar "Harang lila.., dia.. tak
ei mari jala kita.., leka..t di..
'ni ga' mana?"

"Ayu wei.. kundang, kepa..da..
ng hamba apa bala.., denga..n che..
ei taka sial di mana.., maja..l di..
ei mana kita duk champa..k, di pa- ke
 pa..ntai..
laut jangan lagi.. ke ng a..na..k
ah ikan sampah pula.., tia..da..
ei kena sangat lagi.., ke ja..la…
'ni ga' kita."

Oh oh o..h nik o..h
lalu.. wei.. kundang, si cha..pai..
ei pula.., ke ja..la..
'ni kechil duduk champa..k, ke pa..ntai..
laut sangat lama.., seju..lu..ng
lama jawab boleh, tu-de..ng..an
"'Ni kundang ayo tu..an, kepa..da..
ei pantai sial dimana, maja..l di..
mana duduk champak, ke ja..la..
ei kechil jangan sa- sampah pula..,
 tia..da..
ei kena sangat lagi.. ke ja- (c)
sampah pula.., tia..da..
ah kena sangat lagi.., ke ja..la..
ei kechil jangan lagi.. ke ng a..na..k
ng ikan."

Oh oh o..h nik o..h
jawab wei.. boleh, Tok Ra..ja..
ei Besar "Ayo kundang, kepa..da..
ei kami (c) kita gi champak,
 di lu..bu..k
ei besar lubuk besa..r, di ba..tu..
'ni ga' besar."

Oh oh o..h nik o..h
jalan wei.. pula, Tok Ra..ja..
ei Besar dengan pula, si ku..nda..ng
ei dia sangat lama.., seju..lu..ng
lama dua kali, bertu..ju..h
hari dua kali, bertu..ju..h
malam sampai pula, ke lu..bu..k
ei besar lubuk besa..r ke ba..tu..,
'ni ga' besar.

Oh oh o..h nik o..h
lalu.. wei.. pula, Tok Ra..ja..
ei Besar chapai pula.., ke ja..la..
ei Besar duduk champa..k, di lu..bu..k
ei besar lubuk besa..r, si ba..tu..
ei besar sangat lama.., seju..lu..ng
ei lama tarik jala.., si ti..da..k
'ni ga' nga naik.

Oh oh o..h nik o..h
jawab wei.. bole..h, Tok Ra..ja
85 ei Besar "Ng ayo kunda..ng, kepa..da
ei hamba tiba kunda..ng, menye..lam
ah tengok nyelam tengo..k, di lu..buk
ei besar terlungsur pula.., ke ka..ki
ei jala jala leka..t, tu-da..ri..
90 'ni ga' mana?"

[Recording by *Dewan Bahasa*]

Oh oh o..h nik o..h
jawab wei.. boleh, Tok Ra..ja..
ei Besar "Ayo kunda..ng, kepa..da..
ei kami (c) apa bala.., denga..n che..-
ei taka nga duk tari..k, si ja..la..
ei besar jala besa..r, si ti..da..k
ah nga naik a- (c) lekat (c)
jala besa..r, si ti..da..k
ei nga naik lekat pula.., tu-da..ri..
'ni ga' mana?"

Oh oh o..h nik o..h
jawab wei.. boleh, Tok Ra..ja..
ei Besar "Ng ayung kunda- ayo kundang, kepa..da..
ei kami tiba kundang, gi se..la..m
ah tengok, sangat lagi.., ke ka..ki..
ei jala takut leka..t, tu-da..ri..
mana?"

NOTES

Marginal numbers refer to the line of text. Points already commented upon are not further elucidated in the notes; thus, for example, it is not felt necessary to draw attention to the numerous 'filler' words. An asterisk indicates a distortion, intentional or otherwise. The words *kechil* and *pula* in all texts end in a glottal stop.

PAHANG
Ph.1.
5 *ingkang:* Javanese (*ingkang senohon = Yang di Pertuan*). Jidin is unaware of the meaning of this word.
13 *dibantu:* re this use of *di-* where the active is expected, see Sweeney, 1972: 339, 409.
14 *sengkat:* 'as far as', 'up to the limit'.
23 *'ngan:* abbr. *dengan*
27 *segala ... panjang.* In this 'verse' the second and third lines are missing.
34 *sehujung:* * = *hujung.*

Ph.2.
9 *burung barang:* 'any old bird'.
13 *mari:* apparently *beri* is intended.
15 *menantu nga kan* * = (*ber*)*menantukan.*
21 *aib:* pronounced /eʔ/.
39 *padi:* intended is *jadi.*
40 *hitam asap lotong:* stock-phrase; 'devastated'.
45 *rakyat-ayat ten-tentera:* * = *rakyat tentera.*

Ph.3.
A:
5 *royat:* Kel. abbr. *riwayat;* see Sweeney 1972, 338.
15 *Murai:* pronounced /muγei/.
21 *siapa:* pronounced /sapɔ/.
B:
23 *gembéra* = *gembira.*

Ph.4.
A:
6 *Rabi-awal* = *Rabi'u'l-awal; awal* is pronounced /awai/.
40 *berpasal:* pronounced /bɔpasei/.
50 *pukul:* pronounced /pukui/.
51 *Disahut:* after this false start the rhythm of the phrase becomes somewhat confused.
52 *dengan* = *yang.* This usage appears to be confined to her story-telling.
55 *memiah:* equiv. *menyiah* 'push aside'.
57 *berserang:* equiv. *semakin.*
59 *tersunjang* = *tersenjang.*
72 *rabang:* equiv. *rabak*, 'torn', gashed.
87 *Bédar Palembang:* the name of the royal yacht.
B:
51 *deras:* pronounced /deγɛh/.

PERLIS

It may be said of the three Perlis texts in general that:—

(a) in final open syllables, 'a is pronounced /a/.
(b) final 'ar', 'ir' and 'ur' are pronounced respectively: /ã?/, /ĩã?/ and /u?/.
(c) final 'as', 'is' and 'us' are pronounced respectively: /aʰh/, /ih/ and /uʰh/.
(d) final 'al', 'il' and 'ul' are pronounced respectively: /aⁱ/, /i:/ and /uⁱ/.
(e) 'r' at the beginning of syllables is pronounced /ʁ/.

Pr.1.
Of the three performers, Ismail is the most influenced by standard Malay, so that e.g. he pronounces *air* in the standard way (not /aya?/).

A:
2 *sait*: equiv. *sahut*, 'reply'. Apparently, however, the word may, as here, have the sense of *seru* 'call', 'call upon'.
5 *botera*: *apparently = *putera*.
13 *nek*: abbr. *nenek*.
16 *gindang*: according to Ismail, a 'special' word, referring to the coming down of the requested story (see page 13). Mahmud, however, says it should be *ginjang*, meaning the same as *porak peranda* (cf. *genjang*).
25 *Pengkulun*: = *pekulun* ('lord').
32 *Puteri*: pronounced /pətəʁi/.
40 *Dan*: * note this common use of *dan*.
40 *betera*: * = *putera*.
61 *diambil*: see note to Ph.1. (*dibantu*).
80 *nenggara*: * = *negara*.

B:
60 *hasil*: pronounced /hasin/. Thai influence?
67 *serta merta*: meaningless in the context.

Pr.2.
A:
9 *tahun*: pronounced /tøun/. In other parts of Perlis /taun/ and /tain/ are also found.
9 *tak mahu boleh*: 'unable to get'.
10 *disait....dikait*: apparently used synonymously to *niat*, 'made vows'. See also *sait* (Pr.1) above.
33 *nerus*: from *terus*, here 'see into the future'.
43 *'chu*: abbr. *achu*.
67 *mereta*: according to Isahak, from *cherita*. Here, he means 'beyond description'.
73 *daamat*: = *adzamat, damat*, 'noisy'.
79 *meneru*: = *menderu*.

B:
15 *sekenduri*: * = *kenduri*.
18 *Malim*: slip for *Malam*. There are several other such slips, e.g., one line above.
45 *semenajak*: = *semenjak*.
48 *mebunyilah*: = *berbunyilah*.
58 *peturun*: = *turun*.
80 *berdengan*: * = *dengan*.

C:
10 *bernama*: intended is *ulama*.
16 *menyahut*: pronounced /mənut/.

Pr.3.
The use of two dots between phrases indicates that the performer remains silent for the duration of a phrase, although continuing to strum on his *batil*. If no comma separates the dots from a phrase, this indicates that he recites only half a phrase in that instance. It may be noted that in the words *menolak, meniru, ke-, beradu, bernama & berita* the vowel 'e' is usually pronounced /a/.

A:
15 gemita: = gempita.
15 apa: intended is *siapa*. 'No one will want to speak'.
18 kenyeh: 'grin'.
20 kejit: 'wink'.
39 menyala: '*flaming*'.
55 pauh: pronounced /pouh₁/.
66 masakin: = miskin.
77 pi, mai: = pergi, mari.
78 .katur: 'a hollow'.
97 jauh: pronounced /dʒouh/.

B:
21 siapa: pronounced /sapa/.
110 han: apparently equivalent to *hal*. See note on *hasil* (Pr.1.)

LANGKAWI

This excerpt, which is not taken from the beginning of the performance, is chosen because it contains fixed passages, e.g. *orang yang chapik*....

KEDAH
Kd.1.
Abdullah Omar states that he is of Patani extraction, and his dialect gives the impression of being somewhere between the Patani and Kedah dialects. A number of groups in the Sik-Baling areas of Kedah speak a similar dialect. Kelantan-Patani features occurring in this performer's speech are those referred to in my previous remarks (Sweeney, 1972: 295–6) as: (b) ii, iii (exception: *asal*, here pronounced /asai/), iv; (c) i,ii. In final open syllables, 'a' is pronounced both /ɔ/ and /a/, e.g. /lamɔ/ & /lama/. In initial syllables, 'e' (ə) is usually pronounced /ɯ/ (note also /mɯtaɣi/ [*matahari*]). Final 'au' is pronounced /ɔu/, final 'ai' is /e/; final 'am' and 'an' sometimes become /aⁱ/ or /aĩ/, thus: /dahaⁱ/, /malaⁱ/,/sombilaⁱ/, /kɔlaⁱ/ /sipaⁱ/, /dʒalaⁱ/ and /dʒamaⁱ/ for *dahan, malam, sembilan, kolam, simpan, jalan* and *jaman*. In some words this never occurs, e.g. *dengan:* dəɲã/. Of words ending in-*ang*, only in the name *Linggang* is there a shift to /aⁱ/.

A:
2 ga': (Kel-Patani) see Sweeney, 1972: 298.
3 pelapik timang pelapung: opening phrase, not understood by performer.
3 bari: 'story'.
4 be..ei..deru * = berderu.
5 Kuala: pronounced /kɔla/.
12 bernama: pronounced /bəɣinamɔ/.
15 Buding: = puding.
20 menteri: according to Abdullah, *menteri* here means 'consort'.
26 Jong .... Abdullah cannot explain the significance of these names.
31 kechau: according to Abdullah, a type of sea-snail.
38 kundang: here 'visit'.
46 melembung: = melambung.
52 'gong: = agung
58 lerah: according to Abdullah, 'lying on':
67 tajun menajun: 'flowing', of tears.
68 Baapa: buat apa.
68 siapa: pronounced /sapɔ/

B:
4 Talubang: here the pronunciation differs from the first performance. It may be speculated that Teluban in Patani is referred to. There is also a place called Tanjung Luluk in Patani.
40 topang: Abdullah imagined that *topan* 'hurricane' is referred to.
48 timur: obviously *timba* should be used.
50 bersaksi: See Sweeney, 1972: 340.
51 kemudian: pronounced /kumdiã/.

Kd.2.

This dialect is similar to that used in Kd.1. Features in common with the Kel-Patani dialects are those referred to in Sweeney 1972: 295–6, as (b) ii, iii, iv; (c) i, ii. In final open syllables, 'a' is always /a/; final 'ai' is /e/. Final 'ang' veers between /aŋ/ and /æ̃/, thus e.g. /timæ̃ lɛtæ̃/: *timang lentang*, but /don^daŋ/: *dondang*. Final 'am' and 'an' are usually /ă/. *ke-* is pronounced /kɔ/. In excerpts Kd.2 & 3, a hyphen at the end of a line indicates that the performer has split the word with a pause.

A:
- 8 *bedahap* = *penahap* 'corner'.
- 9 *jerung:* 'corner'.
- 9 *jong lapan deksa.* Had cannot explain this. Perhaps *jong* refers to the Javanese unit of measurement.
- 12–25 These two *pantun* are:

  Lepas beremas, beremas pula emas semayang dalam cherana
  Lepas bermaaf, bermaaf pula maaf seorang maaf semua
  and Balas hamba menebas bikung buat sajak ke tengah huma
  Balas hamba menarik Lotong buat sajak tidak kena

- 19 *Balas:* = *bagai, macham.*
- 20 *menebas:* Had pronounces this as *menepas* but insists that the word is *menebas*. He also states that *bikung* is a knife for cutting grass, and that by *sajak, tajak* is meant. *Tengah* is pronounced /təŋə/.
- 22 *menarik Lotong:* 'perform the tale of *Raja Lotong*'. Cf. *tarik Selampit* in Kelantan.
- 31 *Sekin:* = *Miskin*
- 32 *'nuju:* = *menuju.*
- 45 *belang:* equiv. *sambil*

B:
- 7 *bertating nama:* synonymous with *menyebut nama;* a common phrase in the *wayang.*
- 36,42 *ei Sekin:* When asked, Had stated that the absence of the frame-phrase *timang*... was unintentional, and caused by confusion with the melody of *Jubang Linggang.*

Kd.3.

A:
- 3 *lada:* = Kel. *leda,* used in *wayang* phrases with *kejut.*
- 8 *ayu wei kundang:* In 'verses' beginning thus, Had has left out the first line.
- 38 *chetaka* = *jentaka.*
- 75 *tubuh:* a slip for *tujuh.*
- 80 *harang lila:* phrase denoting intensity. In the *wayang* we also find *sara lila.*

B:
- 4 *menyétak:* = Kel. *nyatak* ('double' *ny*): 'sitting up'.
- 14 *timang...:* confusion with *Raja Lotong,* which he performed before this tale.

WORKS CITED

AWANG HAD BIN SALLEH.
    1964   *Selindung Bulan Kedah Tua.* Kuala Lumpur: Dewan Bahasa dan Pustaka.

BIJLEVELD, B. J.
    1943   *Herhalingsfiguren in het Maleisch, Javaansch en Soendaasch.* Diss. Utrecht. Groningen Batavia.

BOTTOMS, J.
    1963   *The Teller and the Tale, a first report on some recent recordings of Malay folk-tales in Trengganu.* Unpublished paper read at S.O.A.S., University of London.

DUSSEK, O. T.
    1915   *Hikayat Pelandok, ia-itu Hikayat Sang Kanchil, Cherita Pelandok dengan anak memerang, Hikayat Pelandok Jenaka.* Singapore.

HAMSIAH BINTI ABDUL HAMID.
    1964a   *Cherita Bongsu Pinang Peribut.* Kuala Lumpur: Dewan Bahasa dan Pustaka.

    1964b.   *Cherita Si-Suton.* Kuala Lumpur: Dewan Bahasa.
HILL, A. H.
    1960   "Hikayat Raja-raja Pasai." *JMBRAS*, 33. 2.
HOOYKAAS, C.
    1947   *Over Maleise Literatuur.* Leiden: E. J. Brill. (1st ed. 1937).

    1961   *Perintis Sastera.* Groningen: J. B. Wolters. (1st ed. 1951).
KLINKERT, H. C.
    1893   *De Pelandoek Djinaka of het Guitige Dwerghert.* Leiden.
MAXWELL, W. E.
    1886   "Sri Rama, a fairy tale told by a Malay rhapsodist." *JSBRAS*. 17.
MEES, C. A.
    1935   *De Kroniek van Koetai, (tekstuitgave met toelichting).* Diss. Leiden.
NIK MAIMUNAH BINTI YAHYA.
    1962   *Cherita Raja Dera.* Kuala Lumpur: Dewan Bahasa.
SKINNER, C.
    1963   "Sja'ir Perang Mengkasar." *VKI*. 40.
SWEENEY, P. L. AMIN.
    1972   *The Ramayana and the Malay Shadow-play.* Kuala Lumpur: National University of Malaysia Press.
WINSTEDT, R. O.
    1927   "The Tale of Trong Pipit." *JMBRAS*. V. 3.
———— & STURROCK, A. J.
    1941   *Cherita Jenaka.* Singapore. (1st ed. 1908).

    1957a.   *Hikayat Awang Sulong Merah Muda.* Singapore. (1st ed. 1908).

    1957b.   *Hikayat Malim Deman.* Singapore. (1st ed. 1908).
WINSTEDT, R. O.
    1958   "A History of Classical Malay Literature." *JMBRAS*. 31. 3. (2nd. edition).
YA'AKOB BIN ISA.
    1971   *Sastera Rakyat dari Pahang.* Latihan Ilmiah Universiti Malaya. (unpublished).
ZAHARAH KHALID.
    1963   *Raja Donan.* Kuala Lumpur: Dewan Bahasa.
ZAHARAH TAHA.
    1963   *Raja Gagak.* Kuala Lumpur: Dewan Bahasa.

NOTE

I wish to express my sincere thanks to my friend Encik Abdul Fattah bin Abdul Karim (L.R.A.M. A.T.C.L., A.Mus.L.C.M.) who sacrificed much time and effort to do the notation of the various tunes discussed in this paper, and also attempted to instil into me some rudiments of musical theory. Needless to say, I accept full responsibility for errors which may occur.

For those interested, I am hoping to make available, in the near future, a cassette of a selection of excerpts from *penglipur lara* tales.

www.ingramcontent.com/pod-product-compliance
Lightning Source LLC
Chambersburg PA
CBHW032142040426
42449CB00005B/370